Your
Horoscope
2023

....

Virgo

24 August – 23 September

igloobooks

igloobooks

Published in 2022
First published in the UK by Igloo Books Ltd
An imprint of Igloo Books Ltd
Cottage Farm, NN6 0BJ, UK
Owned by Bonnier Books
Sveavägen 56, Stockholm, Sweden
www.igloobooks.com

0722 001
2 4 6 8 10 9 7 5 3 1
ISBN 978-1-80108-408-6

Written by Sally Kirkman
Additional content by Belinda Campbell and Denise Evans

Designed by Richard Sykes
Edited by Suzanne Fossey

Printed and manufactured in China

CONTENTS
. . . .

INTRODUCTION
. . . .

This 15-month guide has been designed and written to give
a concise and accessible insight into both the nature of your
star sign and the year ahead. Divided into two main sections,
the first section of this guide will give you an overview of your
character in order to help you understand how you think,
perceive the world, interact with others and – perhaps just as
importantly – why. You'll soon see that your zodiac sign is not
just affected by a few stars in the sky, but by planets, elements
and a whole host of other factors, too.

The second section of this guide is made up of daily forecasts.
Use these to increase your awareness of what might appear on
your horizon so that you're better equipped to deal with the
days ahead. While this should never be used to dictate your
life, it can be useful to see how your energies might be affected
or influenced, which, in turn, can help you prepare for what
life might throw your way.

By the end of these 15 months, these two sections should
have given you a deeper understanding and awareness of
yourself and, in turn, the world around you. There are never
any definite certainties, but with an open mind you will find
guidance for what might be, and learn to take more control of
your own destiny.

THE CHARACTER OF THE VIRGIN

As kind as they are critical, as down to earth as they are successful, Virgoans are the perfectionists of the zodiac. They set ideals for everyone, themselves included, to strive towards. Ruled by Mercury, the planet of communication, they will happily offer their opinions on any given subject, both when asked to and when not. Whilst communicating is a forte for many Virgoans, their sharp tongues and analytical brains can mean that their opinions sometimes come across as being overly critical. Extremely detail-orientated, and with the highest of standards, others can seem to fall short by comparison. However, any criticism Virgoans offer will usually be constructive and full of good intentions.

In opposition to neighbouring Leo, the sign of Virgo belongs to the sixth house, which focuses on health and service. Others often look to Virgoans for help and guidance about dieting or big decisions because they know that they will receive practical, informative and candid advice. Virgoans may well be nicknamed 'Dr Phil' (also a Virgoan!) in their group of friends. As well as giving second-to-none counsel, Virgoans are efficient, resourceful and have exceptional attention to detail. Such strong attributes can help Virgoans to become the highest of achievers, but their humility means they are unlikely to let any success go to their heads. Virgoan superstar Beyoncé, for example, is known for her humble attitude despite her incredible accomplishments and global fame. Symbolised by the Virgin, modest and sometimes shy Virgoans will remain as well presented and orderly as their daily to-do lists. They do not usually opt for anything too showy, as is their more introverted, negative way. Born at the end of summer when the leaves begin to transform in colour, Virgoans are a unique combination of certainty, control and change, which allows them to be both organised and organic.

THE VIRGIN

Not to be taken too literally, the symbolic sign of the Virgin represents many qualities in good, yet sometimes naïve, Virgoans. Astraea, the Greek goddess of justice and innocence, makes up the Virgo constellation and is often depicted as the Virgin symbol. However many compliments Virgoans may receive, they will likely remain modest and could come across as shy, giving them an air of innocence that can be highly attractive. This purity can be why they are often seen as being very prim and proper to the outside world, but their qualities are measured best by their ability to always find the good. Virgoans tend to be fair and true, thanks to their methodical ability to weigh up the facts with intelligence and honesty, much like Librans. Demeter, the Greek goddess of harvesting, is another deity associated with the Virgin symbol. Holding a sheaf of wheat, Demeter is the mother of Earth's fertility and the reason we have seasons, which is perhaps why mutable Virgoans – with their foresight and love of planning – can make wonderful agriculturists.

MERCURY

The speed at which some analytical Virgoans process information is surely inherited from their ruling planet of Mercury, which orbits the Sun faster than any other planet in the solar system. Mercury is named after the Roman god of the same name, who is typically shown with wings on his head and feet. Virgoans are similarly quick, especially when it comes to thinking. However, the speed at which thoughts race around their heads can mean they sometimes overthink things and obsess over the smallest of details. This can make them hold a grudge longer than most.

'Mercury in retrograde' is a phrase that is often met with fearful faces, but what does it mean? Three times a year, Mercury seemingly begins to move backwards and is blamed for many communication, media, technology and travel failures. Whilst many people might avoid making big decisions, signing important documents or arranging trips during a retrograde, ever-practical Virgoans will probably not let their ruling planet slow them down in any significant way.

ELEMENTS, MODES AND POLARITIES

Each sign is made up of a unique combination of three defining groups: elements, modes and polarities. Each of these defining parts can manifest themselves in good and bad ways and none should be seen as a positive or a negative – including the polarities! Just like a jigsaw puzzle, piecing these groups together can help illuminate why each sign has certain characteristics and help us find a balance.

ELEMENTS

Fire: Dynamic and adventurous, signs with fire in them can be extroverted. Others are naturally drawn to them because of the positive light they give off, as well as their high levels of energy and confidence.

Earth: Signs with the earth element are steady and driven with their ambitions. They make for a solid friend, parent or partner due to their grounded influence and nurturing nature.

Air: The invisible element that influences each of the other elements significantly, air signs will provide much-needed perspective to others with their fair thinking, verbal skills and key ideas.

Water: Warm in the shallows and sometimes freezing as ice, this mysterious element is essential to the growth of everything around it through its emotional depth and empathy.

MODES

Cardinal: Pioneers of the calendar, cardinal signs jump-start each season and are energetic go-getters.

Fixed: Marking the middle of the calendar, fixed signs firmly denote and value steadiness and reliability.

Mutable: As the seasons end, the mutable signs adapt and give themselves over gladly to the promise of change.

POLARITIES

Positive: Typically extroverted, positive signs take physical action and embrace outside stimulus in their life.

Negative: Usually introverted, negative signs value emotional development and experiencing life from the inside out.

VIRGO IN BRIEF

The table below shows the key attributes of Virgoans. Use it for quick reference and to understand more about this fascinating sign.

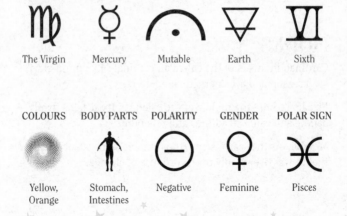

SYMBOL	RULING PLANET	MODE	ELEMENT	HOUSE
The Virgin	Mercury	Mutable	Earth	Sixth

COLOURS	BODY PARTS	POLARITY	GENDER	POLAR SIGN
Yellow, Orange	Stomach, Intestines	Negative	Feminine	Pisces

ROMANTIC RELATIONSHIPS

. . . .

Virgoans can be choosy lovers. They are not often ones to frequently fall in love, but their devotion can last an eternity when finally bestowed on a worthy soul. Anyone chosen by these notoriously picky characters should feel very special indeed. Virgoans can have a tendency to find faults or nitpick about trivial matters, which can be troublesome in love. Wanting to tweak or change minor issues may seem harmless and necessary to mutable Virgoans, but celebrating the differences in their relationships will prove to be far more rewarding than finding flaws. This optimistic outlook of finding the positive needs to extend to themselves too, as they are often left confused as to what their partners see in them.

Although symbolised by the Virgin, Virgoans are not always naïve when it comes to their relationships. They present themselves impeccably to the outside world with lint rollers at the ready, but they can also be extremely laid-back when they feel at ease in a relationship. When they find themselves in the arms of true love, they will no longer worry about their hair being out of place or their clothes being creased. Curious with a mutable nature, Virgoans are often open to trying new things, which can help keep any long-term flames of love burning brightly. They may struggle initially with exposing themselves to vulnerability, resulting in them not always giving their love freely. However, when Virgoans choose to lower their emotional barriers their endless affection can be well worth the wait.

With a deeply rooted earth element, Virgoans will most appreciate partners who enjoy getting outside and who understand the importance of protecting the planet. Eco-conscious and organised, finding someone who will go trekking in the countryside can be just as important to Virgoans as finding a partner who takes the time to separate the plastic and glass for recycling. Chores aside, they will be the most charmed by someone who brings fun and energy into their meticulously planned lives.

ARIES: COMPATIBILITY 3/5

There's not a lot that's similar about how an Arian and Virgoan think and approach their daily decisions. The Arian rushes in excitedly to almost everything, whereas the Virgoan needs to exhaust all the facts and options first. The Arian can teach the Virgoan the benefits of not getting too bogged down with decisions, and the Virgoan can teach the Arian the equal importance of noticing the smaller details in life. When these two team up, they will understand that they are very different, and will likely admire those differences in one another.

TAURUS: COMPATIBILITY 3/5

A Taurean and Virgoan can make for a real power couple. The Taurean's dogged approach to fulfilling goals and the Virgoan's practical and busy mind will see this pair securing a successful future together. The Virgoan can appear overly critical and may end up hurting the Bull's feelings unintentionally. Ruled by Mercury, the planet of communication, the Virgoan can be very attuned to the Taurean's needs and will try to fix any problems within the relationship. These two will likely share many things in common and can form a lifelong companionship, even if a whirlwind romance isn't in the stars.

GEMINI: COMPATIBILITY 1/5

A Virgoan may initially be attracted to a Geminian's charm and wit, but is likely to soon feel irritated by the flights of fancy. The steady Virgoan can feel too reserved for the Geminian, and the fast-paced Geminian can be too unpredictable for the Virgoan. Both ruled by Mercury and strong believers in communication, these otherwise contrasting characters may end up feeling as if they are speaking two completely different languages. However, their mutual love of change and talent for adaptability may well be what makes this relationship last longer than predicted.

CANCER: COMPATIBILITY 3/5

A practical-minded Virgoan could be the balancing force that a Cancerian needs in a partner. The Virgoan will feel loved and protected by the nurturing Cancerian, but by contrast, the Cancerian can at times feel hurt by the naturally critical Virgoan. Thanks to ruling planet Mercury, the Virgoan's strong communication skills should help them patch up any problems. The earth element in Virgo and the cardinal influence in Cancer can make for a driven couple, so any loving ambitions that these two share will likely be realised together.

LEO: COMPATIBILITY 2/5

The love of a Leonian can take a Virgoan by surprise; which isn't something the introverted Virgoan is always keen on. The clear differences between the studious Virgoan and show-stopping Leonian can mean that these two might be quick to write each other off as potential partners at first glance. The relationship between this fire and earth couple can be a slow burner, but their slow and steady approach could well end up with these two winning the race hand in hand. This couple's strengths are their differences, and these two hard workers can make for a solid and complementary couple.

LIBRA: COMPATIBILITY 3/5

Both advocates of diplomacy and justice, a Libran and Virgoan's love should be fair and true. If these two make any vows together, they will take them very seriously. However, it is not all contracts and scales in this relationship, as the Mercury-inspired Virgoan and Venus-ruled Libran could both have a shared love of beauty and crafts. A date night at a gallery or the theatre could be perfect for the art-loving couple. The Libran will have plenty of ideas, and the practical Virgoan could be the one that helps make those fancies a reality.

SCORPIO: COMPATIBILITY 5/5

Positioned two places apart on the zodiac calendar, the passionate and loyal bond between a Virgoan and Scorpian is a special one. The orderly Virgoan will value the steadiness of the fixed Scorpian, and similarly the loyal Scorpian will appreciate the faithfulness that the Virgoan is known for. With their complementary elements of water and earth and their matching negative energies, this typically introverted couple will enjoy the nourishing effects of spending quality time together. Theirs is an intimate relationship but not without some passionate arguments, thanks to the Scorpian's power-ruled influence of Pluto and the Virgoan's sharp tongue.

SAGITTARIUS: COMPATIBILITY 2/5

These two lovers may really have their work cut out for them. Whilst the outdoorsy Sagittarian and earthy Virgoan both have a strong love for being outside in nature, they have some serious core differences. The Virgoan, for example, loves routine, which the Sagittarian can't abide. Elsewhere, the wild Sagittarian, who gallops heart-first towards goals, can sometimes feel too reckless for the overthinking Virgoan. Equally, the Sagittarian might find the Virgoan's overactive mind to be a hindrance. If they can find some common ground, this mutable pair could experience an honest and thought-provoking relationship.

CAPRICORN: COMPATIBILITY 4/5

When a hard-working Capricornian and meticulous Virgoan
fall in love, there won't be many cracks in their relationship.
With the Virgoan's tool kit of practical skills and the
Capricornian's portfolio of material achievements, this
hard-working couple may well be best at taking on grand
projects. Perhaps building their own home somewhere in
the countryside would suit this couple, where their shared
earth element can be appreciated at its best, and their quieter
negative energies embraced. This firm relationship may lack
some spontaneity, so thoughtful surprises now and again could
help keep the excitement alive.

AQUARIUS: COMPATIBILITY 2/5

An idealist Aquarian and realist Virgoan may not be an obvious
match, but this couple can be very happy if they find key ideas
and goals to share. The organised Virgoan will appreciate the
Saturn-ruled part of the Aquarian that represents structure
and order, but less so the rebellious Uranus side that enjoys
throwing out the rulebook. The airy Aquarian and Mercury-
ruled Virgoan are both freethinkers and should be good at
allowing one another room to breathe in the relationship,
which both will value. Ultimately, the optimistic Aquarian and
the pragmatic Virgoan will need to find a shared ambition to
balance out their stark differences.

PISCES: COMPATIBILITY 5/5

Opposites on the zodiac calendar, a hands-on Virgoan and mystical Piscean make a loving match, yet life will not be without the occasional struggle. Water and earth are elements that can create beautiful things together, but in this couple, the emotional Piscean and rational Virgoan could be a tricky balancing act. For example, the Piscean sometimes exhibits an elusiveness that can be attractive or frustrating to the steady Virgoan. Overall, however, these two are deep souls that can empathise and support one another probably better than any other match. They can happily and devotedly serve one another for endless days if flexibility and patience is practised by the pair. A fixed and mutable mode can be a complementary match, so long as Virgoans don't try to bend the will of their accommodating Piscean partner. The bond that these two can share, when at its best, can be sincere and spiritually liberating.

FAMILY AND FRIENDS

· · · · · · · · · · · · · · · · · ·

It's hard to ruffle unflappable Virgoans, which makes them go-to confidants in times of crisis. Their wise words can be second to none thanks to their honesty and practicality, so offering advice to friends and family is a common practice. Whilst the advice of Virgoans will usually be actively sought, their candid tones can sound callous at times. Even if their intentions are pure, their sharp words can penetrate even the thickest of skins. Virgoans might think that their Cancerian and Scorpian friends have hard shells that can withstand straight talking, for example, but they will actually need to tread lightly because both can be extremely sensitive. After a time, even the most patient of people, such as Taureans, might tire of the Virgoan disapproving tone. To avoid alienating their loved ones, particularly their own children, Virgoans should try to always be constructive rather than overly critical, and give any words of advice without condemnation.

Virgoans' homes most likely reflect their impeccable taste. Their style may be minimal, but it will always be warm. They usually function best if their homes are uncluttered, so if their bedroom is looking disorderly it might be an indication that their thoughts are too. Virgoans can often have a gift for cultivating their earth element, so a house with a garden could be an important feature, whether it's to grow their own organic vegetables or prize-winning roses. Outdoor space or not, Virgoans might decide to bring the outdoors in and decorate every room with plants that will all have been carefully selected to clean polluted air or thrive on sunny windowsills.

Not ones for openly displaying their emotions, Virgoans are more likely to silently sulk until their mood passes. Despite holding stubborn grudges that sometimes feel like a life sentence, Virgoans do forgive and forget with time – as their patient and understanding family and friends will know. Learning to move past bad feeling is essential for Virgoans, as the weight of grievances can start to feel heavy after a while. Opening up to loved ones about how they feel, and letting go of any concerns about vulnerability can be an important first step towards mending any broken bonds and forging stronger friendships. Opposites on the zodiac calendar, Pisceans may well be the emotional key to unlocking the deeper feelings lingering inside of Virgoans.

The social circle of selective Virgoans may be small but strong with lifelong friendships. Whilst they love structure, they suit easy-going and energetic signs that challenge and inspire them. Creative Arians can be the best of friends to crafty Virgoans, and their balance of negative and positive energies are a complementary force that makes for a pioneering and practical alliance.

MONEY AND CAREERS

· · · · · · · · · · · · · · · · ·

Being a particular star sign will not dictate certain types of career, but it can help to identify potential areas for thriving in. Conversely, to succeed in the workplace, it is just as important to understand strengths and weaknesses to achieve career and financial goals.

Thanks to their earth element, some Virgoans may be attached to material objects, but these hard-working types are usually more driven by goals than they are by money. Whilst these overachievers could be destined to make fortunes by reaching the top of their professions, many are known for their thrifty spending habits. Finding sample sales and scouring the Internet for the best insurance deals, frugal Virgoans will only part with their hard-earned money wisely and are unlikely to go on a shopping splurge. Their tendency to over-analyse could leave them struggling with indecisiveness and considering the pros and cons on almost every purchase. This means plenty of time should be allowed when accompanying them on shopping trips.

Wellbeing is of utmost important to Virgoans, so careers based around healthy living could be worthwhile. One profession that they may thrive in could be as nutritionists or cooks like fellow Virgoan chef, Melissa Hemsley. However, if chopping vegetables doesn't appeal, perhaps the health calling that speaks loudest to analytical and cool-headed Virgoans is within medicine, such as becoming doctors or surgeons. Most Virgoans love to work in a neat and pristine environment, so the clinical order of a hospital could be exactly what the career doctor ordered. Whether it's for the operating table or the dinner table, Virgoans will need a clean and chaos-free workstation if they are to function at their very best.

Virgoans can be meticulous and they often excel at finding fault, so any occupation that involves careful checking and solving problems will be a good fit. Working as consultants may well be something that Virgoans come to later in life, once word of their shrewd observation and effective counsel begins to precede them. Virgoans should be wary of their perfectionist ways when striving for improvement, however, as wanting to check and double-check everything can lead to some projects never being completed. Practical-minded Virgoans could benefit from practising a more relaxed viewpoint that finished is sometimes better than perfect.

As with family, colleagues cannot be chosen. Therefore, it can be advantageous to use star signs to learn about their key characteristics and discover the best ways of working together. Born in the sixth house, where service can be second nature, Virgoans often excel at both working for, as well as with, other people. Taureans and Capricornians can work doggedly with hard-working Virgoans through the most difficult of tasks, and will bond over their shared grit and determination. Arians, Leonians and Sagittarians are also potentially good workmates, and could help lighten the load with their positive flames by always encouraging their Virgoan colleagues to down tools and take a break.

HEALTH AND WELLBEING

A lack of control can make Virgoans feel anxious, but it is essential that they learn to let go periodically so that they don't make life impossible for themselves and everyone around them. Always ready to give others the best of advice, Virgoans should try to listen to their own wise words. However, seeking external professional advice may also be necessary if their need for control is verging on obsessive. Virgoans notoriously love shopping lists, pros and cons lists and to-do lists, which can quite literally be endless. Writing down worries might free up some mental space for any overactive minds. Learning to take a break may leave Virgoans pleasantly surprised that the world does not collapse when they enjoy a well-deserved day off.

Virgoans can have a reputation for being negative. In some cases this is just them being practical in their unfiltered, candid way, however, sometimes it is a fair assessment and should be mended if it is affecting their happiness. An obvious solution to balance out any negative vibe is to counteract it with some feel-good positivity. Virgoans can become stuck on focusing on the negative and lose sight of the positives surrounding them, but if they take the effort to look around they are likely to be able to find something to be grateful for. It could be family or friends, a good hair day, the Sun shining outside, the rain watering the garden, and so on. Spending time with optimistic Sagittarian friends or family members could also be the positive injection that Virgoans need to boost them on a down day.

Virgoans can be incredibly health conscious, and often take extra care of their mental, physical and spiritual health.

However, sometimes this can verge on hypochondria. Maybe it's because Virgoans are good at noticing the little things that they are so alert to their bodily health, but their internet history is probably littered with online searches desperately trying to self-diagnose the latest potential rash. Scaring themselves with Internet diagnoses is probably a common occurrence, so registering with a local doctor should be the number one priority whenever Virgoans move home. They may well be on a first-name basis before long, but they are always happy to add another name to their Christmas card list. Virgoans generally take such good care of themselves that they should hopefully not have too many reasons to visit the doctor's. Associated with the stomach, Virgoans may wish to take extra care of this area by eating a gut-friendly diet, and easing any anxieties that might be tying their insides into knots.

Virgo

·················

DAILY FORECASTS
for 2022

OCTOBER

. . . .

Saturday 1st

Group efforts are essential today and may have some measure of success. Turn to your family and immediate environment for support in getting something off the ground. Today should be about your friendship circle or significant relationships. This won't leave much time for play, which may upset you.

Sunday 2nd

Your ruler Mercury turns direct now and you could achieve more clarity and understanding of recent relationship problems. You may be challenged to do the right thing and could be inclined to excessive outbursts. Balance will be hard to come by until you've let the dust settle and had space from each other.

Monday 3rd

Conversations are easier today, but you might still need to tread carefully. It may be a case of returning to the beginning and retracing your steps with a different perspective.
You would do well to think of this as a new journey with a new mindset, which has evolved and matured.

Tuesday 4th

A good cause may catch your attention and you could be rushing headlong into a new passion without thinking of anything else. This might make you feel good and raise your self-esteem, but can also be a short-lived or misguided approach to something which isn't really meant for you.

Wednesday 5th

Try to sit still and observe yourself as an outsider. It may help to ground you and take in the bigger picture. You may be anxious or impatient if you can't do things your way. Use your methodical mind to analyse what is going on for you. Get all the information and filter it.

Thursday 6th

You could drop into a dreamy and floaty mood now. Partners may enjoy and encourage this. However, you must be sure to stay as realistic as possible, as there's a risk that you avoid or neglect your daily duties. Be of service to each other with unconditional love and support.

Friday 7th

A sudden change of tactics could result in a romantic or creative project being scrapped or transformed into a masterpiece. You may have a continuous flow of ideas and wish to get practical today. Your instincts might tell you what needs to be improved on or discarded completely.

Saturday 8th

Enjoy connecting with your inner compass today, but be mindful that you could still be harbouring false hopes and delusions. You might need a reality check before making any commitment to new plans. By evening, you may find that something is bigger than you and feels too overwhelming for you to tackle alone.

Sunday 9th

Pluto turns direct now and is done switching things up in your romantic and creative zone. A full moon may highlight your efforts of self-discovery over the last six months. Stay alert to what occurs today as you might receive an important revelation about your personal work or artistic projects.

Monday 10th

Check your deadlines today, as there could be something that has sneaked up on you and needs completing now. Be astute and check every tiny detail of important issues. You could be more driven today and have your sights set on reaching your goals in the shortest time.

Tuesday 11th

Treat yourself to something nice today. Schedule quality time for yourself with good food and company or simply an early night with your favourite TV show. You might be processing thoughts about finding a better home and work balance, and you may like to begin implementing that this evening.

Wednesday 12th

Your mood could conflict with your duties today. There may be a lot to do and you simply can't be bothered. You may prefer to stay in a state of bliss but have practical work to do. Take a mature approach and get all your chores done, then relax with a clear conscience.

Thursday 13th

Your productivity is higher now and you may be putting in more effort or making up for lost time. Use your mind and be discerning if you can. You could be learning something new or managing others and need to use your negotiating skills.

Friday 14th

Compassion and harmony are your goals now. It might be part of your job to maintain good relations with clients or seek out connections in the wider world. Find it within yourself to be a good listener and show empathy where it's needed. Be respectful and responsible with elders.

Saturday 15th

It's possible that something has touched your core and you have an emotional attachment to it. This might be something you've learned recently, and you could now decide to be more proactive about it. Friends and social groups provide the outlet you need to feel safe, nourished and loved.

Sunday 16th

Stay in your safety zone today and feed your soul. Maternal figures may be helpful, and you may wish to connect with family members. You might also return to childhood treats or have nostalgic conversations. There's no need to do anything much today except enjoy a day off.

Monday 17th

You could start to feel guilty and believe that you've wasted a weekend. Use this precious time to take care of your basic needs. However, you may also feel vulnerable or exposed and wish to be alone now. If romance or creativity isn't forthcoming, keep it for another day.

Tuesday 18th

There may be an issue which you have to confront today. Muster all your inner courage and speak only your truth. People may notice that you've found your voice and you could be attracting an audience. If this is unwanted, you could be able to express yourself another way.

Wednesday 19th

You could experience some challenges today, which can set you back and upset you. Check in with yourself as these may be triggering old wounds or childish habits that no longer serve you. It's possible that you're reacting and not responding in an adult manner and this is causing tension.

Thursday 20th

Take a deep breath, as there's better energy today and you may be more successful. You may find a balance between expressing your essential needs and being productive in the workplace. Someone may have heard your plea and has taken steps to make you feel more comfortable about being assertive.

Friday 21st

The moon in your sign may help to bring you back to your centre and become calmer. You could be spending the day making a lot of connections or checking out details regarding travel and education. Allow yourself to tentatively plan a break or holiday. Making an itinerary will satisfy you.

Saturday 22nd

You may not feel like being with others today. Wrap yourself up in your studio or workspace and do what you do best. Creative or personal research might excite and energise you. A good clear-out will allow you to see what is taking up space.

Sunday 23rd

Saturn turns direct today and you may find that your mundane duties and obligations ease up now. Be prepared for intense love connections. Someone or something has piqued your interest and you may feel things you haven't experienced for a while. Investigate this exciting new opportunity.

Monday 24th

Your head and heart are in sync now and you might be following up on a lead which adds quality to your life. This could be a good cause, a community project or a role in which you can excel and be of service to others. Be sure not to take on too much.

Tuesday 25th

A new moon and solar eclipse give you the green light, telling you to go ahead. Whatever has presented itself as a potential source of enjoyment has come at the right time for you. This may also be something mysterious and seductive, which can meet your personal needs.

Wednesday 26th

Let go of what can never be and look towards the future now. Don't let things hang on to your energy and spoil your good mood. You may need to have harsh words with someone who refuses to back out of your life. Stay calm and be kind and respectful.

Thursday 27th

You have the right kind of energy to pursue a new dream today. It may be that you have newfound inspiration and are fired up to do something with it. Take your time, as you should know by now that you are better when you have a plan and follow the steps.

Friday 28th

Jupiter returns to your relationship zone for a brief period. This may hint that you have unfinished business to deal with. A legal matter may come up to be reviewed. It may also be that you have a renewed optimism and faith with a relationship or important person.

Saturday 29th

Home and work duties may clash today, or you could be burning the candle at both ends and suffering for it. Mercury jumps into your communication zone and heats up the action currently going on there. However, remember that you must go slowly and take in all the information.

Sunday 30th

Mars turns retrograde now. This influence will help you to stop charging into new things. You may be more discerning and think twice before adding your energy to something which may potentially drain you. Today, however, you could be excitable and look forward to a clandestine meet-up with a mysterious person.

Monday 31st

You may have found your muse now and can put all your effort into making gold from lead. Your creative exploits may grow larger or become more profound. You could even be adding a taboo or occult aspect. Do be careful what you say to others, as it could be frowned upon.

NOVEMBER
....

Tuesday 1st

Take everything with a pinch of salt today. The energy
suggests that you might become very frustrated or irritated
by little things. This is a passing mood and you would do
best to listen to the advice of your elders and not overstep
the mark in all areas.

Wednesday 2nd

Your mental abilities may be slow-going and confusing.
Remember that you must slow down now and skim things
back to manageable sizes. You may desire to switch off and
forget about things this evening. Unwinding with a partner
can help you to let go and relax. A love issue from the past
may return.

Thursday 3rd

Today you're more light-hearted and whimsical. Perhaps
you've drifted to your fantasy island with a lover. Conversation
and romance flow easily and merge into one. Your wants and
needs are in sync. Enjoy this momentary pause of bliss before
the energy amps up again.

Friday 4th

Today you must keep one foot on the ground and try to stay
grounded. You could be at risk of wandering off and never
coming back. You can connect with your inner compass, but it
still holds elements that aren't real. Check in with your body
or do some practical activity.

Saturday 5th

Here is your chance to let go of any karmic baggage you've been carrying around for a long time. You might have had a visit from the past recently, but you can now deal with it once and for all. Romance and creativity can be both exciting and annoying.

Sunday 6th

You might be inspired to do something great for the wider world. However, you may need to think smaller and realise your limitations. Conversations are karmic, and you could be signing a deal which completes a legal or financial transaction. It's best not to try and attempt to control something you don't understand today.

Monday 7th

The energy may feel heavy for you today. There's a hint of espionage, secrecy and underhand dealings. Stay away from this and concentrate on personal pleasures. Put ideas for travel or higher education on a vision board and expand your horizons. This may be something you can do next year.

Tuesday 8th

A full moon and lunar eclipse close a window of wild card energy. This can entice you to spend more than you can afford and indulge more than you should. Listen out for subtle messages from your ruler who may divulge a secret or two. Prepare for an upgrade in your communications and contacts.

Wednesday 9th

Put your money where your mouth is or stay silent. You may be at risk of speaking out of turn or coming across as foolish. There is volatile energy around and you would be safer if you lie low and stay out of trouble. Don't overindulge on the good things in life.

Thursday 10th

You may be stubborn today and could clash with someone in authority. Your ability to read between the lines may expose a fake and cause some tension. Let yourself have a dreamy, floaty afternoon with loving or sexy messages to and from a lover. However, don't be taken in by falsities.

Friday 11th

It might be tricky to meet someone in the middle today. There may be a standoff and you could refuse to budge. This isn't going to move anytime soon, so look at things from a different angle. You will need to be humble and agree to compromise.

Saturday 12th

A weekend with your friendship group could be calling you. It might be that your wider social circles have events going on that you're interested in. Alternatively, an evening with a lover can be emotional, sensitive, sharing and caring. Good food and company are the flavours of the weekend.

Sunday 13th

This is a lovely day for feeling safe, protected and nurtured.
Friends and lovers could be involved, but so can maternal
figures. You may wish to do things which remind you of your
childhood. Stay grounded and don't let nostalgia get the better
of you. Conversations with siblings can be uplifting and joyful.

Monday 14th

Whatever emotions you begin the week with can feel
exaggerated today. You may notice that you feel happiness and
sadness together which can be confusing. If you need time
this afternoon to process this, be brave and express yourself
somehow. Art or poetry might help you do this.

Tuesday 15th

Don't get carried away with secret messages to a lover.
Although this may feel good, you may need to get a reality
check. The sooner you do this the better. You could be floating
on cloud nine but need to get on with hard work and practical
activities. Find a balance now.

Wednesday 16th

If there's something you need to say to someone, do it today
because the energy is about to shift, and your focus will
change. Take advantage of the moon in your private zone to
express intense and intimate feelings. A leap of faith is needed
to share your deepest desires.

Thursday 17th

Family now becomes your main focus and there might be plans to be made. This is where you shine as a leader and you could be rallying the troops in preparation for celebrations. Try not to neglect your duties here as there may not be time to catch up later on.

Friday 18th

Take things slowly again today. You could be pushing against the flow in work, travel and your relationships. This can feel overwhelming and you may need a break to see to your own needs. Make it known that you will be available after you've seen to your own needs.

Saturday 19th

Today you must aim for balance. Check your finances and look around your home. Is there anything that needs to be freshened up or given a new lease of life? Family members may pull together on a DIY project that brings more lightness, laughter and harmony your way.

Sunday 20th

Keep plugging away at anything that you started yesterday. By evening you might have a better sense of who are your friends and allies. It may be a case of serving others while also having favours returned, and this can make you feel good. Acknowledge that some people have different skills to you.

Monday 21st

You have another chance to express deep feelings to someone special. It might be that you've upgraded a relationship status and have moved on to a new level. This may feel strange if you decide to go public with it. Sweet words of love, encouragement and support are offered by family.

Tuesday 22nd

The emphasis is now on your family of origin and you may be leading the way or hosting parties. A nagging feeling of leaving something behind may bother you, but it is for your ultimate benefit if you can let it go with love. Grieve your loss if you need to.

Wednesday 23rd

Dreams and visions you've shared with another may be a topic of conversation today. Be careful because the energy suggests that you may be being unrealistic again. Remember that your inner compass is still retrograde and is asking that you realign when you know exactly what you want.

Thursday 24th

A new moon in your family zone lets you set intentions for the next six months. There may be a big project that you can all be involved with. This may involve truth-seeking, going the extra mile and broadening your horizons. Jupiter turns direct to emphasise this.

Friday 25th

You may feel extra tired today and look forward to the weekend. High energy may have drained your batteries recently and you may now need to unwind. However, there's still work to be done, just do it slowly and methodically with frequent breaks to recharge yourself.

Saturday 26th

You might enjoy a day of resting or doing something creative. This is also a nice day for catching up with people you haven't connected with for a while. Short and long-distance friends may appreciate you checking in on them. There may also be homework which needs completing soon. Meet your deadlines before the holidays.

Sunday 27th

Dedicate some time today to pursue things that you alone are interested in. These may involve making space for something new or putting down ideas for creative projects you have in mind. Take your time with these as they are seeds to plant another time.

Monday 28th

You are more outgoing today and willing to do overtime to complete your mundane duties. However, you may hit a roadblock. This could be your personal energy that is flagging. Only do what you can and don't commit to anything more. Delegate your chores or politely refuse others if you need to.

Tuesday 29th

Look after yourself better today as you may still be exhausted. Give yourself some love and compassion or speak to family members who can help to relieve you of your obligations. You may find that an elder or boss is willing to give you a hand. Know your personal limits today.

Wednesday 30th

Partner time is highlighted as this may be your best way of unwinding and recharging. A lover may know exactly how to get you to stop doing so much and to let others do things for you. Phone calls and messages can wait another day as you could need to rest.

DECEMBER

....

Thursday 1st

Listen to your intuition today and hold on to your inner compass. This might be a time of pause for you to realign and get things straight in your mind. Outside challenges can be ignored or put to one side whilst you recuperate and find your place again.

Friday 2nd

Your emotions may be larger than usual, but this can act as a catalyst for a big change deep within you. Introspection and truth-seeking could bring you some revelations about your inner workings and the mysteries of life which fascinate you. You could be putting some puzzle pieces together today.

Saturday 3rd

Be open-minded now. You might feel outgoing and more optimistic, but your energy may be lacking. Take this time to nurture yourself and gather your family around you. You may be inspired or likewise be the inspiration for someone following a similar path. It could be your turn to guide someone else.

Sunday 4th

Neptune turns direct now. All will become clearer very soon. You may have already had a glimpse of this. Don't push for answers, let them come to you naturally. Take a day off hard work and overthinking, and allow yourself some pleasure. Good food, company and travel documentaries may suffice.

Monday 5th

You might feel as if there is something you need to expand on now. This is possibly a relationship issue, and you may need to open your mind just a little more. There is an air of irritation around you, but this could also be excitement and anticipation.

Tuesday 6th

Your family may need more attention today. Perhaps your wisdom is needed to negotiate or solve a small problem. Keep all lines of communication open and clear. You could be planning events which are in line with your dreams. Try to be flexible as you might be the one hosting or organising these.

Wednesday 7th

Be mindful of the energy today as it's deceptively peaceful. This may afford you time to research or make enquiries about projects you're passionate about. Your ruler is now in your creative and romantic zone and can amplify your need for knowledge of the right steps to be taken.

Thursday 8th

A full moon meets Mars today. It could illuminate where you're stuck or need to slow down. It may also highlight the completion of a work project which has been going on for some time. Congratulate yourself on this. You may receive a reward or bonus from a boss or authority figure.

. . . .

Friday 9th

Friends and social groups might require your company this weekend. You may not wish to spend more time with them than you have to as you have other projects in mind. You could be dismissive of others and prefer to look after your own needs. Protect your energy today.

Saturday 10th

Both love and creativity may get a boost from Venus today. It's possible that you put a lot more of your soul desires into your art. You may also be realising that the way to success is to be good to yourself. Start by reading the rule book and following the steps.

Sunday 11th

Feelings of vulnerability may surface and trigger a few old wounds. These could be about your self-esteem, and you may doubt your talents or romantic prospects. However, these are because of the shift within you, and you would prefer not to expose your personal path to friends just yet.

Monday 12th

You may be conflicted today. On the one hand, you might want to tell the world what you intend to focus on now. On the other, you may be protective and defensive as a way to avoid any kind of criticism. Be brave and tell one or two close friends.

Tuesday 13th

Don't let anyone put you off or tell you that you aren't good enough. These may be your deep-seated fears and they could be triggered today. Own your part in the collective and stand up for what you believe in, including your human rights. Being witnessed is important to you.

Wednesday 14th

The moon drops into your sign and you gain confidence. Practical applications can show you that you are valued and can give you a boost. You may begin planning how to woo someone with your art and dedication. Beauty is in the detail and you, more than most, understand this.

Thursday 15th

Heavy earthy energy can help you to stay grounded and focused. You may find that time drags in the workplace, but this acts as a bonus and you can get more done. Find out everything you need to know about travel, learning and connecting with others for the upcoming festive period.

Friday 16th

Don't be scared to take a leap of faith today. You might need to jump right into something to fully understand it. This immersive experience may give you the answers you require or the impetus to investigate further. If it adds quality to your life, then go ahead and leap.

Saturday 17th

You could be putting aside your personal projects and running a long list of chores today. This will be fine if you take it slowly and prioritise. You could get an unexpected surprise from someone you may not have heard from in a while. Enjoy catching up with them.

Sunday 18th

Try to find a balance between your mundane chores and your own agenda today. It may be difficult to find time for play, but you are doing the right things and joining in with groups to arrange, coordinate or plan a gathering. Stay mindful of any health issues today.

Monday 19th

The energy amps up to an intense level where communications need to be probing and precise. There may be many options for you to choose from or filter. It could be that you have deadlines to meet and you need to be razor-sharp with your attention to detail.

Tuesday 20th

Jupiter returns to your intimacy zone and you may be thinking about continuing your quest for inner knowledge. First, you must leave something behind. This could be that you delegate or discard a duty, but can also be that you adjust a dream and make it more attainable.

Wednesday 21st

The winter solstice brings you a day of reflection. The shortest day ushers in the darker nights and you must sit, pause and give gratitude for the year gone by. Think about the love that surrounds you and the inspirational people you include in your circle. Your creative projects may become more profound in this season.

Thursday 22nd

The festive activities may be taking their toll on you and your energy could be lower than you'd like. It's important now to do what's important for the greater good and come back to your personal goals when you have a clear mind and more strength.

Friday 23rd

A new moon is the perfect opportunity to set your goals and intentions regarding art, expression and romance. You may have learned not to rush these things. Making a plan, a to-do list or a schedule for the new year would be an excellent activity now. This will be beneficial in the long run.

Saturday 24th

Today you may be more loving and sociable. As the season dictates, you could be spending time with a loved one and sharing dreams and visions. You might be co-creating or having a pleasurable, cosy time together. Conversation and love flow easily and feel mature and responsible now.

Sunday 25th

Today it's important that you exercise self-control, as you may be tempted to excesses, which can lead to feeling unwell. Take it easy and be open to sharing and expressing love and happiness. You may find that others are attracted to the joy and optimism you show.

Monday 26th

If you feel tired, you must rest. If you feel irritable, then withdraw from potentially problematic situations. You might have overdone things yesterday and now need to pull back. You may be commended for being responsible and knowing your limits. Be an example to others in your circle, especially the young ones.

Tuesday 27th

Indulge in special time with a partner and switch off from the outside world in your own way. It's okay to dream and drift to a fantasy island now. Enjoy a surreal time of love, co-creation and connection. You may feel more attuned spiritually today and give thanks for your blessings.

Wednesday 28th

If it's possible to continue relaxing and feeding your soul, then do so. You may get a boost from your inner compass and confirmation that your way is now clear. It might now be more obvious where you're meant to be heading for your personal growth in the coming year.

Thursday 29th

Mercury turns retrograde today and reminds you to keep your wits about you. You could be reviewing decisions made regarding love and expression and ensuring they are in alignment for you. Big gestures of love and soul-searching may need to be taken with a pinch of salt for now.

Friday 30th

You may be anxious to get on with things but still lack energy. Listen to your body now and stay in a place of low activity. Your mind may also be doing overtime thinking up new schemes or plotting how the next year will pan out. Give it a rest today.

Saturday 31st

The energy today is heavy, and you may wish to decline any spontaneous invitations. However, you could just be stubborn and decide to bring your celebrations closer to home. Do what you love and enjoy your evening.

Virgo

....

DAILY FORECASTS
for 2023

JANUARY

. . . .

Sunday 1st

Your thoughts could turn to the past as the new year begins.
You may be remembering someone lost to you. Ritual is a
wonderful way to honour the past. To do so at this time of year,
with its theme of endings and new beginnings, is special.

Monday 2nd

Communication is a key theme as the new year begins. In
particular, you may be reminiscing with your loved ones about
the past or be finding out more information about a new
love interest. This is an ideal time for exploration rather than
action. Feel your way slowly into 2023.

Tuesday 3rd

Try to keep emotions out of the equation, especially at work.
Use your clever mind to help you find solutions to problems
and focus on working as a team with your colleagues. Be
logical and rational. Don't be tempted to speak your mind any
more than is necessary.

Wednesday 4th

Focus on your health as 2023 gets underway. Try not to put
yourself in a situation that is stressful or demands too much
of you. Aim to keep a healthy balance in your life. When in
doubt, focus on the positives and the things that are working
well for you.

Thursday 5th

This week's full moon is about considering what you enjoy in life and where pleasure lies. Turn your attention towards self-expression, your skills and your talents. Are they fulfilling you and do you get the attention you want or deserve? If not, it might be time to realign your goals.

Friday 6th

There's a get-real factor to your stars, especially around the areas of romance and love affairs. Have those all-important conversations and decide whether you want to recommit to a dream, a hope or desire. The more you put into life, the more you receive in return.

Saturday 7th

The full moon can be a time of clarity and today's alignment promises illumination and insight. Sit and meditate early morning, or line up a significant conversation over lunch. If you're concerned about a lover or child, you may learn something new that deepens your understanding of them.

Sunday 8th

Try something new to change a situation for the better. This might be linked to the way you talk to a child or lover. What you say may surprise them, but could help reopen the lines of communication. Don't push for change, however, as a natural turning point will come in ten days.

Monday 9th

If you're looking for a new romantic relationship, you may meet someone on your daily commute or at your place of work. Create a strong sense of camaraderie in the office or wherever you spend your day. Working alongside other people amicably and efficiently is the ideal scenario.

Tuesday 10th

If you're bored of your job or routine, you'll feel it this morning. You know you're in the wrong situation when your energy levels are low and you're constantly tired. Change is coming, so make a wish list or draw up some new goals. Engage with what you want to do differently.

Wednesday 11th

Being a Virgo, you're one of the earth signs, and this is where there's strong planetary energy. You're at your best when you draw up a plan and work steadily towards it. This is an ideal time to consider what brings you pleasure and plan something exciting for the year ahead.

Thursday 12th

Action planet Mars has been retrograde in your career zone since the end of October 2022. You may have experienced a period of unemployment, or the opposite and you've been overwhelmed or stressed with your work. Now's your chance to get on track and take back your power.

Friday 13th

Other people are a key part of your happiness, but it's wise to keep firm boundaries in place and not give more than you receive. Who makes you happy and what needs to change if you want to be with one person more? Think of this period as the time to explore your emotions fully.

Saturday 14th

You may decide to invest in your health today. This could mean you join a gym, buy some supplements or change your diet. As a Virgo, your body and health are important to you and you're often closely attuned to the mind-body-spirit connection. Think holistically.

Sunday 15th

If you're currently in an unconventional romantic relationship, this may not sit easily with you. You could decide to knock a flirtation or romantic liaison on the head if it impacts your work or your health. Alternatively, you may realise that the other person's not ready to commit yet.

Monday 16th

It's likely to be a day of strong emotions, especially if you've found out what someone close to you is grappling with. Be there for other people but try not to be overly critical or play the blame game. There are usually countless reasons why a relationship falters and you may not know all of them.

Tuesday 17th

Words have power and current events are your cue to take back control and be in charge of your destiny. This could mean standing up to someone in a position of power or refusing to do what someone says. If you've been bossed around, decide whether it's time to issue an ultimatum.

Wednesday 18th

Communication planet Mercury turns direct in your romance zone. You may hear from someone who's been quiet for a while and an on-off relationship could be back on again. There could be good news regarding a child or a creative project. Take the initiative and be proactive.

Thursday 19th

Recent events may have illuminated where you're wise to let go and move on. This could show you what's working well in your life and what's not. Be clear about which projects you want to continue with and which you want to get rid of. A new work phase is about to begin.

Friday 20th

The Sun enters your work and health zone today. This turns your attention towards your routine and lifestyle and how you can be of service to others. This zone is closely linked with your star sign. The more you have a routine that works for you, the more content you are.

Saturday 21st

Today's new moon spells good news if you want to apply for a job or start a new habit or health routine. Use online technology to make your life easier. Learning to be flexible and multitask can help you move forwards. You might have to change holiday dates to be accommodating.

Sunday 22nd

Pay close attention to the basics of life and work at getting these right. Boost your fitness, tweak your eating habits, find regular employment or create more order and structure in your everyday life. Look at what makes you happy on a daily level and do more of it.

Monday 23rd

Teamwork benefits you now as it makes life easier and more enjoyable. Focus on collaboration rather than competition, think less about yourself and consider everyone's needs. It's a good week to help create a harmonious working environment, wherever you spend your days.

Tuesday 24th

An early start isn't ideal if you're lacking sleep. You could be unusually argumentative and quickly get on the wrong side of someone you work with. Try to avoid a tense situation. Where your life looks rosy is in a personal relationship. It's an ideal day to connect with children or lovers.

Wednesday 25th

There may be a reason to celebrate today if you have a new job or you're promoted or get a pay rise. Work and money matters are in sync and a little bit of good fortune could come your way. Adopt a positive attitude at work and you could help to improve your company's prospects.

Thursday 26th

You're wise to do what you can to boost your finances while you have the best planet Jupiter in your resources zone. Line up some new goals to earn money or to invest what you have. This potential wave of good fortune could continue for the next few months.

Friday 27th

The best news for you this week is the fact that Venus enters your opposite star sign Pisces today where it remains for the next few weeks. As Venus is the planet of love and Pisces rules your relationship zone, this promises romance. Lose yourself in a magical love affair.

Saturday 28th

It's a gorgeous weekend to prioritise love, travel and good times. If you're away on holiday or visiting somewhere new, this is when a romantic relationship could flourish. If you're single, make the most of life and book a spontaneous trip away. Sometimes, life encourages you not to plan.

Sunday 29th

Your stars are urging you to expand your horizons and be open to new experiences. If you're on a workshop this weekend or learning a new skill, you're in tune with your stars. Be open to an alternative lifestyle or pursue a unique or unusual activity. Embrace your weird.

Monday 30th

Put your personal life to one side and focus on work and ambition. It's an excellent day to get ahead and pursue a new work project or goal. If you currently have two jobs, you're in sync. It's an ideal time to ensure that you have more than one string to your career bow.

Tuesday 31st

When it comes to your working life, you're likely to favour a fast-paced environment where you can use your communication skills. Your career stars are being powered up over the next couple of months, so make the most of this. Be bold and ambitious and utilise your natural abilities.

FEBRUARY

. . . .

Wednesday 1st

The focus remains on your work and career today. You might be firming up your next steps, or you want some reassurance that you're on the right path. Thorough preparation and attention to detail are required before you can impress the boss or share your ideas with the world.

Thursday 2nd

Your connections are your biggest weapon at work. It's not who you know but how you treat one another that matters. Work your people skills today and create some tight bonds in your life. A romantic lunch date could hit all the right spots. Be loving and giving to others.

Friday 3rd

Try not to compare yourself detrimentally to other people today. Everyone's different and it might be the right time for you to review your personal skills and talents. If you say the wrong thing today, you may feel bad. If in doubt, nod knowingly and keep your thoughts to yourself.

Saturday 4th

You may want some time out this weekend. If you can have a couple of days of self-care and pampering, go for it. If you've been busy with work, prioritise your health and wellbeing. Your confidence might need a boost, so be around the person who lifts your spirits.

Sunday 5th

Kick back today and create some time and space in your life for quiet contemplation. Today's full moon is ideal for looking at your situation carefully to see what you may need to release or let go of. Don't rush through life, but slow things down so you can make a clear decision.

Monday 6th

Your love life is under the spotlight as your ruling planet Mercury teams up with romantic Neptune. This is gorgeous for losing yourself in love, even if it doesn't favour clear and honest communication. You may hear promising news about a child's new romantic relationship.

Tuesday 7th

The moon is back in your star sign, which often means you feel more emotionally stable or settled. You might experience some challenges at work, however, if you clash with your boss or another employee. Trying to get your needs met could be almost impossible today.

Wednesday 8th

Love planet Venus teams up with live-wire Uranus today. This is gorgeous for being spontaneous in love. Line up a special event with your other half, perhaps a holiday or trip away. Ring the changes and do something different. You could be asked out on a date unexpectedly.

Thursday 9th

If you're typical of your star sign, you're not usually a big spender. Yet you can still fall prey to the lure of retail therapy. If you're keen to spend, start by making a list of what you want to buy rather than making impulsive purchases. If it's beautiful or brings you joy, it's probably right for you.

Friday 10th

You might be continuing with a daily discipline, a hobby or a craft and want to pursue it devotedly now. There may be key areas of your life that you want to focus on, for example, childcare or romance and love affairs. Throw yourself wholeheartedly into life's pleasures.

Saturday 11th

Your ruling planet Mercury changes star sign today and enters Aquarius, which rules your work and routine, your lifestyle and your health. It's in these areas where you're wise to get organised and manage your time well. It would be a good date to start a fitness or health journal.

Sunday 12th

You may want to socialise today and get to know new people. Say yes to a community event or catch up with the neighbours or people close to home. Yet superficial chit-chat won't do it for you. You're more interested in getting to know other people on a deep level.

Monday 13th

You may not see eye to eye with someone you work with today. They might be overly rational or intellectual about a project you're involved in, whereas you feel passionate about what you're doing. Try not to let other people's opinions stop you from pursuing the life you choose.

Tuesday 14th

You may be delighted if you receive a Valentine's card this morning. If you're a parent, why not send one to your child. Romance is in the air, although you could end up discussing practical or financial matters with your partner. Today could tick more than a few boxes.

Wednesday 15th

If you were hoping for a romantic experience this week, today looks gorgeous for a romantic lunchtime meal. This is when the love barometer is off the chart and wildly romantic. Later on, you may find that family or domestic issues kick in, dampening the love vibe.

Thursday 16th

Don't take on too much work and don't despair if you're struggling to find any. If you are under the cosh at work or suffering with a health issue, take the time to make any adjustments or significant decisions today. This could mean saying no to extra responsibility and taking care of yourself.

Friday 17th

You're one of the earth signs, with oodles of down-to-earth common sense. This may be what's needed during a weird and wonderful Pisces vibe. Who's telling the truth and who's telling lies? Cut through the fantasy and get down to the nitty-gritty of a relationship.

Saturday 18th

You're strongly influenced by other people now, or you have someone in your life who's a strong attraction. This person could be good for you, or they could lead you astray. Be wary around anyone who likes to lead a fantasy life.

Sunday 19th

Your relationships are either going to be completely wonderful or confusing and disorienting. It is up to you to take self-responsibility and work out what's best for you. The promise of a fresh start is always alluring but you're not usually one to lose yourself in a heady romance.

Monday 20th

Today's new moon falls in your relationship zone. This indicates that you may be able to start over when it comes to love, or perhaps you're about to sign and seal a joint venture or new business partnership. Team up with the right people in your life and you can go far.

Tuesday 21st

Be aware that things may not go according to plan today, especially at work or on the road. The current planetary line-up can feel like a Mercury retrograde phase. Therefore, be willing to be flexible and adaptable and double-check everything if you're travelling or signing a contract.

Wednesday 22nd

It's an excellent day to walk your talk and do what you say.
Communication planet Mercury and action planet Mars align
in your work and career zones. If you want to impress a person
in a position of influence, choose this evening to make your
mark. This could benefit you financially.

Thursday 23rd

Whatever you're discussing or negotiating this week, it has the
potential to be a lucrative deal. Aim high and value yourself
highly. You may have key information at your fingertips that
could prove to be a winning formula. This might spell good
news for a legal or financial matter.

Friday 24th

You could be spending a lot of money but try not to feel
resentful and give generously if you can. It's a lovely weekend
to head off to pastures new. You may be visiting family or be
introduced to the in-laws. If you would benefit from some
alone time, make it happen.

Saturday 25th

As an earth sign, you often delay gratification to get what you
want in the long term. This isn't your best mode of action
now, especially when it comes to travel or study. What favours
you most is to leap in spontaneously and sign up for a new
workshop or a course abroad.

Sunday 26th

You can sometimes drop yourself out because you get caught up being of service to others or taking on other people's responsibilities. Think twice today before you say yes to a request for help. If you cover for someone at work, make sure you're doing it for the right reasons.

Monday 27th

It's a positive day to meet up with a powerful person who can help you financially. This may be an influencer, a recruitment consultant or a financial expert. Use your connections to boost your career today. Stay on track with what you want to achieve and don't procrastinate.

Tuesday 28th

If you're negotiating money matters, know your worth. There's potential for you to do well now but you have to sell yourself. You may have a unique talent or skill that means you're indispensable. This could help you negotiate a new role or position or a high-flying job.

MARCH
· · · · · · · · · · · · · · · ·

Wednesday 1st

Make sure you complete what you've started. Firm up the details of a negotiation and ensure that a contract is signed and sealed. Once you know that everything is in order, then can you start celebrating and consider how you're going to spend the money that may be coming in.

Thursday 2nd

Communication planet Mercury enters your relationship zone today. Therefore, you know that there's going to be plenty to talk about, either with a significant one-to-one in your life or a business partner. If you're looking for love, you could meet someone new from a different country or culture.

Friday 3rd

Be wary around your friends today. Someone could be envious of what's happening in your life and try and sabotage your plans. If in doubt, don't reveal everything that's going on. Depending on what takes place, you might decide to have a quiet night at home this evening.

Saturday 4th

You may want to shut the door on the world this weekend, not because you're feeling upset but because you have a lot going on. If you're working on a new money-making project, it's worth changing your plans last minute if you're on a roll. Do what feels right for you.

Sunday 5th

You could be working on a project, plan or presentation today. One way or another, you may have to impress someone in a position of influence in the week ahead and it's worth being prepared. You could have some tough critics, so even more reason to know your stuff inside-out.

Monday 6th

This could turn out to be an eventful week for you, primarily because today's full moon takes place in your star sign, the only one this year. If you have reason to be proud of yourself, celebrate in style and make sure you congratulate yourself on a job well done.

Tuesday 7th

Other people remain important in your life during this week's full moon and perhaps more so than usual. You might have to rely on others in a new capacity. Don't be afraid to hand over the reins where necessary, especially to someone who complements your own skills.

Wednesday 8th

You may decide to put your partner before yourself today, or perhaps you're aware that you're relying too heavily on another person to support you. Yet this is the time to get the right people on your side to boost your prospects moving forwards. You can't do it all by yourself.

Thursday 9th

Be around people whose ideas and success rub off on you.
If you want to improve your finances, hang out with a wealthy
crowd or arrange a meeting with an influential person.
You may have to brag about yourself today or show off your
true worth. Don't be shy – just do it.

Friday 10th

It's worth pushing hard today if you know you're on the verge
of sealing a deal or landing a new job. Aim to impress and use
your persuasive abilities to get what you want. Sitting back
and waiting for the world to come to you is not the best policy.
Make the most of your success stars.

Saturday 11th

Pisces rules all forms of partnership in your horoscope and
Mercury in Pisces loves to talk about love. If you want to
talk to someone special about a trip away or a holiday or
you're keen to book a course, it's an excellent date to make a
spontaneous move. Make good connections.

Sunday 12th

If you're typical of your star sign, you have a way with words
and you can be extremely persuasive. Use your communication
skills to a good advantage today, whether you're counselling
someone younger or giving out advice. Say yes to a community
event close to your home.

Monday 13th

If someone in your family or a person you live with is having a hard time with things, be there for them. An early morning conversation could help them get back on track, or at the very least, be the support they're looking for. Tackle a domestic project with enthusiasm.

Tuesday 14th

Take a step back from career matters today, especially if you're feeling disillusioned about your next steps. Try not to let your imagination run away with you. It's not a great date to mix business with pleasure. Don't discuss work with a loved one if you have different ideas about what's right.

Wednesday 15th

There's a magical element to love this week. It's a great day to be with someone special in whichever way works for you. If you're feeling disillusioned, however, do what feels right and don't give in to someone else's wants or needs. Try not to put other people before yourself.

Thursday 16th

It's important to have an honest conversation today, even though that could be a big ask. You may want to hide the truth from someone close or not hear what someone else has to say. A partner's declaration could be hurtful, whether this applies to your personal or professional life.

Friday 17th

Love and romance are all well and good but it's also important to consider the practical side of a relationship. If you're in love with someone who's a disaster with money, it's time to confront the issue. If you want more commitment and financial stability, push to get your needs met.

Saturday 18th

You may spend some of the weekend catching up with a work project or dealing with administration online. One area you're wise to keep on top of things is money. This is where your astrology is peaking, so make a plan for your financial strategy.

Sunday 19th

Communication planet Mercury moves into Aries today and your joint finance zone. This is a good time to talk things through with your other half, or check up on your investments. Whatever works for you in your current situation. Be proactive around money and act fast.

Monday 20th

Money is under the cosmic spotlight this week as the equinox takes place today: the Sun's annual move into Aries, the first sign of the zodiac. Therefore, it could be a time when you're discussing finances with someone close. Money and love are linked. Dive deep into a taboo issue.

Tuesday 21st

Today's new moon is gorgeous for taking the initiative and starting something new. You could receive money or a gift close to this new moon, or feel compelled to help someone out. Set your intentions around earning money, investing money or putting your money towards a good cause.

Wednesday 22nd

Use the forward-moving vibe of the new moon to your potential and ask for what you want or need. It's an excellent date for negotiation or lining up some new investments. If you're talking about property, you're in tune with your stars. Consider your long-term future carefully.

Thursday 23rd

Today's theme is power and you could hear about a take-over bid at work. Do whatever you can to make sure that you're not the one in the firing line. If you're worried about your job or current position, you may decide to postpone a holiday. Ensure this is the last resort.

Friday 24th

Your stars are gorgeous for a holiday romance and, hopefully, you've escaped any dramas at work. If you're still lusting after a person you met abroad, it's an excellent time to reach out to them, or leap on a plane and turn up unexpectedly. Bring some excitement to your love life.

Saturday 25th

Action planet Mars is on the move today leaving behind your career zone and moving into your friendship zone. As long as you have other people to lean on and convince you that you're doing the right thing, it's a positive period to embrace the new and find a different path in life.

Sunday 26th

You might need some reassurance today if recent events have left you feeling insecure or unsure of your next steps. If a company recently changed hands or went out of business, you may have to start over in some way. It may not look like it right now, but you could be better off financially.

Monday 27th

It's a good day to negotiate finances. If your finances are flush, consider how to make the most of your money, especially if savings rates remain low. Property investment could be a great side business for your star sign, but think carefully and consult experts first.

Tuesday 28th

A lot depends on your current situation but you seem to have a knack of looking at things from a fresh perspective. This could help you make money or come up with new ways to deal with your situation. An unexpected gift or bonus could land on the table.

Wednesday 29th

Focus on the bigger picture in life and line up a new adventure. If you can get your friends on board with what you're planning, even better. If you're married or in a long-term relationship, it's a good idea to arrange to spend some time with your partner's best friends.

Thursday 30th

Go with whatever schemes or dreams you like the sound of, especially if they're creative, artistic or fun. If you're a parent, line up a trip or adventure with your kids. If you're looking for love, think about your foreign connections or check out someone you meet in a place of study.

Friday 31st

If you can take the pace slow today, make it happen. You might take the day off if you can afford to do so. A lot seems to be going on internally and you don't want to miss any important insights or intuition. Write in your journal or meditate and tap into your inner wisdom.

APRIL
· · · · · · · · · · · · · · · · ·

Saturday 1st

You might feel deflated if one of your best friends is heading off on holiday and leaving you at home. Try to look on the bright side and think of the money you're saving. Your turn will come before too long. Get those travel brochures out and find yourself a bargain.

Sunday 2nd

You may be looking for the person to reassure you that what you're doing is right today. It's unlikely to be your other half but could be a good friend. However, it's worth asking yourself why you're not willing to stand firm and back the strength of your convictions.

Monday 3rd

Your ruling planet Mercury is on the move today as it enters earth sign Taurus. This is your travel and study zone. It's an ideal time to start looking out into the world and consider the bigger picture. Religion, beliefs, ethics and your spiritual path are part of this.

Tuesday 4th

When planets are in Taurus, you invariably start to look beyond the everyday and want to explore life to the full. You could be frustrated if you're trapped at home or you've decided not to spend money on a holiday. Now might be the time to change your mind about what's possible.

Wednesday 5th

Sit down with your other half today and consider whether you can afford a holiday together. It's important to be sensible about money but, at the same time, you don't want to miss out on creating new experiences together.

Thursday 6th

Today's full moon is about money for you. It's an ideal time to balance the books, review your finances and include other people in your calculations. Fairness is essential, so do your best to sort things out amicably. This may be necessary because of a sudden change at work.

Friday 7th

If you're in a relationship or married, you could be pleasantly surprised today when your partner books a holiday or a trip away for the two of you. It's a lovely evening for romance so make the most of this, whatever your current relationship status. Talk to someone new.

Saturday 8th

You may not give up until you get what you want. If you're trying to plan a holiday or a trip away, today is great for persuading your friends to travel with you. You might have to be flexible and change your ideas of what makes a great holiday but either way, go for it.

Sunday 9th

You might be dealing with someone in your life today who's unhappy or depressed. You care about other people deeply so reach out to help, whether this is in your local community or with a member of your family. Don't forget to pay attention to your needs as well.

Monday 10th

The moon is in your home and family zone today and this may be where your attention lies. It's at home or within your family where you want everything to be harmonious and sorted. Tick a few things off your to-do list as you're likely to get busier quite soon.

Tuesday 11th

The planet of connection, Venus, moves into your career zone today. This is about finding the right people to partner with to further your future goals now and over the next few weeks. Get the right people on your side and you can go far. Look to your friends for support and inspiration.

Wednesday 12th

Your current astrology signifies a windfall, a cash bonus, a gift or a return on investment. It's also a wonderful time to gift other people. You may have taken on a big financial commitment recently, but the end is within sight.

Thursday 13th

If you're a parent, it's a known fact that children can cost a lot of money. If you're paying out on a student loan or for educational purposes, put your Virgo fact-finding ability to good use and make sure that you've got the best deals. The more organised you are now, the better.

. . . .

Friday 14th

Today's astrology suggests that a working relationship is a no-go zone. In other words, don't mix business with pleasure. Keep your working relations amicable and put any ideas of romance out of your head. You may need to budget carefully if you're buying work clothes or school uniform.

Saturday 15th

If you're offered overtime or work experience today, it's definitely worth your while saying yes. Money and work are linked, and showing willingness could open the door to abundance. Step into a volunteer role and this could lead to a paid position further down the line. Work hard, be diligent.

Sunday 16th

Today looks lovely for your close relationships. Meet up with your best friend or spend quality time with your other half. There's an easy flow and a chance to get a relationship on a more even footing. If you want to bring love, understanding and openness back, here's your opportunity.

Monday 17th

If you're a typical Virgo, love is one area of your life where you sometimes forget to engage your common sense. You can be idealistic about love and get carried away on a fantasy. Hopefully, you've learned to be emotional without losing yourself. Today could put the theory to the test.

Tuesday 18th

This would be an ideal time to delve a little deeper and ensure that you're swimming in the world of money rather than circling around it. Learn to play with money and enjoy your money as much as possible, whether you have lots of it or not enough. Identify your money motivators.

Wednesday 19th

A new eclipse cycle begins this month, which highlights money for you. Eclipses tend to bring what's hidden to light, which is why it's important to be cash savvy. As eclipse symbolism is shadowy, this might be about an aspect of money that's a potential blind spot. Tread carefully.

Thursday 20th

A solar eclipse can coincide with a wake-up call. The best-case scenario is that today's eclipse comes with a bonus, an investment, an inheritance or a gift of money that comes your way. Certainly, it's a good time to team up with other people to attract abundance into your life.

Friday 21st

There's some big astrology taking place this week. This might mean closing the door on a money deal that's not working out or stopping a financial plug so you don't lose out. As this impacts your travel and study zone, it's here where a lack of cash could impact your choices.

Saturday 22nd

You may not like it if your other half is working this weekend. However, if a work opportunity comes your way, you won't think twice about saying yes. If this affects your holiday plans, you could still choose to prioritise work over play. Changing circumstances require a fast response.

Sunday 23rd

Communication planet Mercury is retrograde in your travel and study zone until mid-May. If your plans have changed more than once, focus on what's working out rather than giving too much energy to what's not working out. Team up with a colleague to boost your career prospects.

Monday 24th

You might have to console a friend today if they got caught out during this period of change. Be there for people you care about as long as they're not calling you up in the middle of the night. Ideally, catch up with a friend this evening and concentrate on your work during the day.

Tuesday 25th

You might need reassurance from your partner today, or perhaps you're discussing future plans. Use the timing of your astrology to postpone a holiday or course for a few weeks. This will give you the opportunity to explore all your options. Something better could come along.

Wednesday 26th

There's a possibility of an argument if you feel misunderstood by someone close to you. Be aware that this is a time when it's hard to get to the bottom of things and miscommunications are likely. Also, you probably have different ideas about money, what's realistic and what's not.

Thursday 27th

The outcome of the next couple of days depends on whether you enjoy your own company or not. You may enjoy thinking things through alone and like to create time and space to listen to your intuition and insights. As long as you don't fall into negative thinking, you'll be fine.

Friday 28th

If you're typical of your star sign, you are something of a worrier with an overactive mind. Try to actively engage in relaxation techniques to restore sanity and calm. You may not react well when things go wrong but be persistent and do your best to stay upbeat.

Saturday 29th

You may be feeling out of sorts and not want to be around other people. If your confidence has recently taken a knock, this could be why. Later on, you're back in the swing of things when a good friend knows how to put a smile on your face.

Sunday 30th

If someone's let you down recently, pay more attention to what you want out of life. Return to your wish journal and spend time on your personal goals and aims. A relationship setback doesn't mean you have to give up your dreams. Reorient your compass and look to the future.

MAY

. . . .

Monday 1st

Consider letting go of an old habit, a job or the old way of doing things so you can move forwards. Otherwise, you may feel your work or health is going backwards. It's worth staying up late tonight as you could have a brilliant insight about a trip or course. Engage in magical thinking.

Tuesday 2nd

Spend time balancing the books and make sure your finances are in order. You might be dealing with a large amount of money or a major transaction. If you're planning a sabbatical or extended holiday, start a savings plan and work out how much you can put away each month.

Wednesday 3rd

If you're typical of your star sign, you like order. That doesn't necessarily mean you're super tidy, but you do benefit from having your work and finances organised. This helps you to have a strong base in your life and firm ground under your feet. Tempers could flare this evening.

Thursday 4th

There's a creative influence to your stars but be wary of a person who could lead you astray. Ensure that you lose yourself in a good way and tap into your dreams and imagination to inspire you. Be careful of falling into a pot of emotions that leads you nowhere.

Friday 5th

Today's full moon lights up your learning zone so consider where you want to be more creative in your life. It's said that your star sign was born to serve and this is true. Yet Virgo rules crafts so make a commitment to learning a new skill that will benefit you moving forwards.

Saturday 6th

Your plans could change suddenly this weekend as trickster planet Mercury remains retrograde. Ensure that you double-check travel arrangements and paperwork more than once if you're on the move. Allow yourself extra time to get from A to B. A night at home may be preferable.

Sunday 7th

Today's stars are a reminder that all work and no play doesn't lead to a fulfilled life. Reorient your compass moving forwards and line up some social events. Love planet Venus is tickling your friendship zone. If there's someone you want to get to know better, make it happen.

Monday 8th

You don't have your work hat on today and you'll be happiest if you've got an extra day at home. You might be feeling wistful about love and find it hard to stay focused. This evening could bring some excitement around money or relationships when you step out of your comfort zone.

Tuesday 9th

Your adventure zone is being stirred up once again. This is about wanting to do things differently and needing more to life than the everyday and mundane. Pursue your personal dreams and line up something different or alternative. Refuse to let go of your dreams and make a plan.

Wednesday 10th

Tempers could rise today if you don't see eye to eye with a good friend. You won't enjoy being around someone who moans all the time. Make sure you're not the one who's being overly critical. If people choose to do things differently, it doesn't mean that they're wrong.

Thursday 11th

Events today may make you realise where you're missing out. If someone at work is talking about their holiday or exciting study plans, this could spur you into action. Go back to the drawing board and have another think about an opportunity that didn't work out the first time around.

Friday 12th

If you want to join in with a group of friends and be offered an invitation to an event, this is not the time to sit on the fence. Be careful not make out that you feel unwanted. Alternatively, line up your own trip and invite the friends you choose.

Saturday 13th

It's a great day to pursue a relationship or deepen your connection with a friend. Make the right moves and you could receive a promise or commitment that you didn't see coming. If you're going to a wedding, it will not only be enjoyable but spark your romantic interest too.

Sunday 14th

It's a lovely weekend to focus on romance and close relationships. If you're in a relationship, be spontaneous with your other half and do something special together. If you're looking for love, consider joining a dating app. When the stars are aligned, it's worth making the most of your love prospects.

Monday 15th

Communication planet Mercury turns direct today. This may bring new information to light that helps you make a clear decision moving forwards. Mercury is in your travel and study zone. There might be news from someone who lives abroad and it's a green light for foreign connections.

Tuesday 16th

Jupiter's change of star sign today is important for you. Over the next twelve months, you may find your wanderlust kicking in or you have a burning desire to broaden your horizons. If you want to live abroad, take a sabbatical or go back to studying, here's your opportunity.

Wednesday 17th

These are the areas of life that are in the foreground while the planet of opportunity Jupiter moves through Taurus: travel, learning, philosophy, the meaning of life. Your focus is on the future and what's next. Look ahead, work on your dreams and goals and live life to the full.

Thursday 18th

You might be less work-oriented and keen to experience more from life now. You could make a radical move and give up the day job to pursue a big adventure. Money and status may be less important for you moving forwards as your attitude to life shifts.

Friday 19th

Today's new moon highlights your travel and study zone, lending you an ideal opportunity to say yes to a new path ahead. If there have been some big changes bubbling away in your life, this weekend is perfect to set your intentions and take the initiative with your plans and ideas.

Saturday 20th

This is a good weekend to trust your intuition and listen to your inner voice. Focus on your personal or spiritual development and work on your confidence. This could be a pivotal time for you regarding your career or vocation. Don't put up with being second best, aim for the top.

Sunday 21st

You could be feeling fired up and ready to take on the world. If someone's annoyed you at work recently or you've had a health scare, you may be aware that life is short and you're not going to be taken for granted. Start by talking yourself up and know your capabilities.

Monday 22nd

You'll fare best at work if there's fresh impetus and a new project to get your teeth into. Otherwise, you could get bored. Being around other people is a key part of your satisfaction. This is not the time to work alone or be too solitary in life.

Tuesday 23rd

Be around the colleagues or friends who stir your imagination and stoke the fire in your belly. This is a good time to be ambitious, step out of your comfort zone and say yes to life. Don't stand back and watch other people's success without making a strategic and brave move yourself.

Wednesday 24th

As a Virgo, you can let other people take the lead and play a supporting role instead. Life's calling you out now to do things differently. Turn your anger into passion and work hard to boost your confidence and self-esteem. Be less critical of yourself and proud of what you've achieved.

Thursday 25th

The more you learn to control your mind and be in charge of your thoughts, the better. Take a course in neuro-linguistic programming or cognitive-behaviour therapy, and explore some new ideas or therapies. Your next big step in life starts with believing in yourself.

Friday 26th

Love and travel are linked today. This could mean you're enjoying a holiday romance or you hear from a lover who lives abroad. If you're in a relationship or married, consider booking a holiday or romantic trip away. Get together with a friend and line up some fun adventures together.

Saturday 27th

The moon's move into your sign means it's an ideal time to work on personal goals and enjoy some 'me time'. A few hours of quiet and writing in your journal may benefit you. Your other half might be disappointed but do what's right for you.

. . . .

Sunday 28th

If you're typical of your star sign, you take your responsibilities and commitments to other people seriously. The trick now is how to hold on to those responsibilities without dropping yourself and your goals out of the equation. Start by making a compromise and meeting halfway.

Monday 29th

Try not to let guilty feelings hold you back. You like to make other people happy but you can't do it all of the time. Right now, your stars are encouraging you to realise your ambitions and make an independent move. The less you rely on someone else financially, the better.

Tuesday 30th

You may feel more emotionally stable when you're in a good financial position and you enjoy your job or work commitments. Use your clever brain to negotiate well today and ensure you end up in pole position. Your positive attitude can rub off on other people – manage that team well.

Wednesday 31st

Put work before love today and concentrate on making a good impression. If you're out shopping or bidding in an online auction, ensure you stay within your budget. It would be easy to get carried away, especially if a good friend is egging you on. Consider trading skills or talent.

JUNE
. . . .

Thursday 1st

Widen your social circle close to home and this could benefit
you in all kinds of unexpected ways. You might meet like-
minded people or be able to create a support network that
helps everyone involved. Find out what's going on in your local
community and neighbourhood.

Friday 2nd

Don't believe that you have to do everything on your own and
delegate key tasks at work or home. If you're a typical Virgo
who likes to do everything by yourself, now's an ideal time to
change your tune and start asking for more support. Meet up
with a friend this evening.

Saturday 3rd

This weekend's full moon highlights the foundations of your
horoscope. You might be reconsidering the work/life balance
and realise that you're trying to take on too much. Your heart
lies with family while your head lies with work. Aim to balance
both and meet in the middle.

Sunday 4th

Your ruling planet Mercury is active during today's full moon.
This could lead to a spontaneous decision around travel
or study, doing what you think is right on the spur of the
moment. It's a good time to gain the counsel of your most
trusted friends, the ones who know you best.

Monday 5th

As the week begins, it would be a good time to check up on someone who's been quiet recently. Be there for other people and be of service where you can. Leave your ego out of the equation and try not to let strong emotions get in your way. Be selfless and true to your Virgo nature.

Tuesday 6th

Your mind could be super creative today. Write down your ideas and don't dismiss them, even if you think they're crazy or alternative. If you're a parent, make time to listen to a child and hear what they have to say. If they want to pursue an unusual career path, be encouraging.

Wednesday 7th

If you're involved in a romantic liaison at work, it might be best to knock it on the head for a while. What starts as a light flirtation could develop into a deep obsession. Alternatively, you could be the one who ends up counselling a colleague about their love crisis or relationship drama.

Thursday 8th

This isn't a good time to reveal everything, especially when it comes to affairs of the heart. You're wise to keep your feelings to yourself for numerous reasons. You might inadvertently upset someone if you're treading on their toes romantically. Also, your feelings could chop and change.

Friday 9th

If you're in a long-term relationship or married, make time for love this evening. One of you may need more commitment or reassurance so spend some quality time together. If you're single, a new love adventure could take you on a roller-coaster ride throughout the summer.

Saturday 10th

There are a few warning lights that suggest mixing business and pleasure isn't wise. You don't want to damage your status or reputation and this is a time when you could do well at work. Be clear about where your priorities lie and address any issues directly this evening.

Sunday 11th

Your ruling planet Mercury is on the move this weekend as it enters Gemini, the star sign at the peak of your horoscope. Gemini rules your career and vocation, your status and reputation. This is a positive symbol for clever ideas and quick moves that can help you on your future path.

Monday 12th

Open the lines of communication and get things moving at work. This is especially important if a job or contract has recently come to an end and you're looking for a new role. It's an ideal time to juggle two jobs or have two strings to your bow. Prove you can be flexible and adaptable.

. . . .

Tuesday 13th

There might be another reason why you want to do well at work. If you're a parent, you may need extra money to support a child or you have a hobby you love but that's expensive. Work out a plan that sees you through the end of the year.

Wednesday 14th

It's an ideal day to book a holiday or sign up for a study course. Embrace freedom and take a big step on your own. You may want to get away from an emotional issue that's confusing you. Sometimes, when you change your surroundings, this helps you change your perspective.

Thursday 15th

This is a time when you may have to speak up, however radical or controversial your thoughts. You can't be happy with yourself if you don't say what you're thinking, especially if this is about world events and the society you live in. Your world might also be your place of work.

Friday 16th

Other people may be looking to you to take the lead at work. There could be a mini-rebellion taking place against a boss or someone who's not pulling their weight. Your colleagues will turn to you for your ideas and advice. Trust what you have to say and stay late if necessary.

Saturday 17th

Get the right people on your side today. You may lose the support of an influential person, or perhaps you hear that someone who's been giving you a tough time is out of the picture. Try not to get too caught up in other people's lives and keep sight of your goals and plans.

Sunday 18th

Today's new moon is great for starting over at work or within your career to initiate a new project or plan. Notice where in life you're in your element and do more of it. This might include communication, either the spoken or written word.

Monday 19th

If you're stepping up in the world, you're likely to come across other people who don't see eye to eye with you. If so, try and learn to become immune to criticism, or at least don't let it stop you from achieving what you want. Have faith that you're moving in the right direction.

Tuesday 20th

You can't please all of the people all of the time but you'll know who's got your back. Align yourself with the right expert, adviser, solicitor or boss. You will soon have the support you're looking for, even if one person has let you down. Shake off the bad vibes and move on.

Wednesday 21st

It's an excellent day to walk your talk and show off your unique skills or talents. Don't let imposter syndrome get in your way and dare to fake it till you make it. The Sun's move into your friendship and group zone is great for networking and getting the support you need.

Thursday 22nd

You have to be wary over the next few months that you don't let your caring nature stop you from living the life you choose. It would be easy to miss out on an adventure because you want to be there for your partner or take on a caring role. Notice who or what's calling you today.

Friday 23rd

It's a lovely day to line up some new social plans. Extend your circle and make some new connections. As the moon is in your star sign, the ball's in your court to reach out to other people. One friend in particular may be waiting for you to be in touch.

Saturday 24th

It's an ideal weekend to be setting off on holiday or visiting another part of the country. If this coincides with a trip to visit friends you haven't seen for some time, you're in tune with your stars. If you're in a relationship or married, step out on your own for a change.

Sunday 25th

Love could be interesting. You may feel passionate about love, or you start feeling irritated with someone close, question your love and feel confused. This is par for the course so go with the flow for now and don't make any assumptions based on what's happening.

Monday 26th

Be careful that you don't turn any anger in on yourself today. Any frustrations are best expressed healthily. This isn't the best time to get involved in a debate about politics or cultural differences. Tempers could flare quickly. Take a step back or count to 10 before reacting.

Tuesday 27th

If an old friend gets back in touch with you today, reply immediately. The more good friends you have on your side now, the more supported you're going to feel. It's important to have someone you trust who you can confide in about a personal issue or a romantic situation.

Wednesday 28th

You may have a lot that you want to talk about today. Dive a little deeper into your emotions and voice some of what you're feeling. It will help to hear another person's opinion, especially if you're finding it hard to make sense of things. Turn to a coach or counsellor for support.

Thursday 29th

If you're in a relationship but there's a lack of commitment, don't be in denial. It's important to let your other half know what you're thinking as they may have similar feelings. Not talking about a personal issue won't help matters, because you close the door to finding a mutual solution.

Friday 30th

If you're feeling overwhelmed trying to keep too many different balls in the air, give yourself a break and take some time out. Also, this might give you some welcome breathing space if one relationship is demanding a little too much of you on an emotional level.

JULY

Saturday 1st

Collaboration is the key to your success today, working alongside other people rather than trying to do everything on your own. There could be good news for a friend, or perhaps you're celebrating a friend's birthday in style. Say yes to a music festival or group get-together.

Sunday 2nd

Encourage someone close to open up and try not to be shocked by what you hear. Remain open-minded. It's a time when secrets could emerge and you're right to encourage other people to dig deep to reveal hidden motivations and tell the truth. Be brave and bold in your interactions.

Monday 3rd

Today's full moon lights up your social zone. This offers you a chance to look at your friendships more closely and decide where change may be needed. Also, it's a key time to draw up new guidelines regarding your children or in a group situation. Trust your instincts.

Tuesday 4th

If a child in your life has become quiet or withdrawn, don't ignore what's going on. You might have to delve a little deeper and be persistent if you want them to open up. This is where your compassion may be needed, so engage your caring nature. You might be working late.

Wednesday 5th

It's time to kick into Virgo mode, which means it's an excellent day for being efficient and getting organised. Whether you're busy at home or in the office, create online systems that work for you and get on top of administration or correspondence. Make time for some socialising, too.

Thursday 6th

You may develop FOMO today and have a fear of missing out on what's going on. Try not to let what's happening in other people's lives distract you and stay off social media if necessary. Focus on the task at hand and take good care of your health and body.

Friday 7th

As an earth sign, you crave solid relationships in your life and like to know where you stand. If you're unsure of someone's feelings, don't try and second guess them today. If you're feeling anxious about a relationship, let someone know you need reassurance. Ask for what you need.

Saturday 8th

There's a serious waft of romance coming your way this weekend. Make time for a close relationship and dive deep into loving connections. It's easy to let a long-term relationship become mundane, so prioritise some sweet moments for yourself and the one you love.

Sunday 9th

Your ruling planet Mercury teams up with romantic Neptune today. This is a heartfelt combination, whether you're writing poetry or texting 'I love you'. Breathe life into your hopes and dreams and use visualisation techniques to help you. Be kind to others and ask for the same in return.

Monday 10th

Action planet Mars enters your star sign today. Decide where in life you need to step up your game to be seen or heard. Start by confronting someone close if you're worried about their ongoing behaviour. Try not to turn a blind eye to anything untoward.

Tuesday 11th

Your planet Mercury is on the move and enters your secrets zone today. Keep some issues to yourself and don't think that you have to reveal everything. Inner work, meditation and relaxation will serve you well over the next few weeks. Dive in deep and listen to your inner voice.

Wednesday 12th

You may decide to change travel or study plans because the timing doesn't feel right. Alternatively, life could step in and set you on a new path. Tune in closely to your inner motivations and trust your instincts. Do what feels right rather than what you think is right.

Thursday 13th

You need to plan your mode of attack at work carefully.
If there's someone you don't get on with, try not to get into
an argument and keep your opinions to yourself for now.
There's a danger that your dissatisfaction could leak out and
damage your reputation or even your job.

Friday 14th

Keep things on the straight and narrow at work and try not to
rock the boat. In your social life, look out for a friend who's
caring and kind. Also, see what occurs regarding travel or
study. Events could open up unexpectedly and you'd be wise to
accept a last-minute invitation.

Saturday 15th

If you're worried about what's happening at work, stop for
a while and do something else entirely. Your social zone is
buzzing this evening so ensure you line up a fun event and
hang out with your friends who know how to make you laugh.

Sunday 16th

When you have the right group of friends in your life, it can
feel as if anything's possible. Catch up with the people you
love the best today and put the world to rights. You'll quickly
realise that everyone has some problem or issue to deal with.
Together you're bigger and better.

Monday 17th

Today's new moon highlights your friendship and group zone.
You may have people you want to meet up with, or perhaps
you're engaged with a group of people who bring excitement
your way, either on- or off-line. It's an ideal date to turn to a
new page and start over with a good friend.

Tuesday 18th

You might be catching up on sleep today if you had a social weekend. If you're feeling tired, cancel a few things in your diary so you can recuperate and recharge your batteries. It's an ideal day to indulge in self-care and some personal pampering.

Wednesday 19th

Work on your mindset today, whatever this means for you. You might want to boost your confidence or say affirmations out loud. Write in a journal about all the things you love about yourself and your life and start practising gratitude daily. Self-love can be hugely beneficial.

Thursday 20th

You might be up against tough opposition or be dealing with someone close who's having a tough time with things. Try to remain compassionate in all your relationships. If you're the one who needs advice or support, a good friend could step in to save the day.

Friday 21st

Action planet Mars is currently in your star sign, powering you up and adding vitality and energy to the mix. This can be an angry Mars but a passionate one, too. Certainly, you're going to feel strongly about things. Don't let other people blur your instincts of what's right and wrong.

Saturday 22nd

Your emotions may be intense this weekend. If one relationship in your life has been difficult recently, you could find that the truth emerges now. It's important to dig deep within yourself to see whether there's anything you need to do or say to help you find a resolution.

Sunday 23rd

Love planet Venus turns retrograde today. This can be a time when deep passions and inner desires emerge. Getting involved in a relationship could feel dangerous or illicit. That doesn't mean it's wrong. It's for you to decide what's right depending on your personal situation.

Monday 24th

You're wise to tap into the side of your nature that's flexible and adaptable today and find your rhythm. As a Virgo, you can sometimes get set in your ways but this won't serve you now. If you're feeling anxious or worried, use your top tips and tricks to calm your mind.

Tuesday 25th

If life took a dramatic turn at the weekend, give yourself some time and space to allow your emotions to settle. There may be something that you want to say or speak about. You could try this evening but it's not going to be easy, especially if someone close refuses to listen.

Wednesday 26th

Be true to yourself now and put your needs first. Keep your ideas under wraps and don't give everything away. There's a theme of secrets and privacy in your astrology. It's a good time to consider your feelings without having to share them with everyone concerned.

Thursday 27th

Perhaps you've developed feelings for someone close that has to remain secret, or the two of you are parted. Either way, it looks as if you have a lot to think about and you're learning at a quick rate. Your personal growth or development could sky-rocket during this time.

Friday 28th

Your ruling planet Mercury enters Virgo this evening. This is the ideal weekend to focus on your personal goals and aims, your image and your profile. Put yourself and your physical wellbeing first. Arrange a makeover or begin a daily habit that benefits you.

Saturday 29th

Pampering would be a lovely way to tune in to your stars. Book in a massage or beauty treatment and prioritise your wellbeing and self-care, as long as you don't line up cosmetic treatment or a radical makeover or haircut – that wouldn't be wise while Venus is retrograde.

Sunday 30th

Create some quiet time for you this weekend and engage in journalling or some serious chilling out. If you're in a loving relationship, the two of you may enjoy doing nothing in particular. The best relationships are when you can be silent and don't feel obliged to talk.

Monday 31st

Hopefully, you're feeling more relaxed after the weekend.
If you can, keep the slower pace going as the new week begins.
Focus on all the things in your life that bring you pleasure and
do more of them, for example, a walk in nature, a leisurely cup
of coffee or playing with your kids.

AUGUST

· · · · · · · · · · · · · · · · ·

Tuesday 1st

Today's full moon highlights your work and health, your lifestyle and your routine. This is about being of service to others at the same time as you focus on your wellbeing. Care for yourself first, others second. Be adventurous this evening and try an activity you've never dared do before.

Wednesday 2nd

Who or what is saying no to you? It looks as if you may be up against a wall of silence today, or a person of authority who's denying your wishes. You may have great powers of concentration so use your clever brain to further your interests rather than bang your head against a brick wall.

Thursday 3rd

It looks as if you have some opposition in your life, whether this is personally or professionally. As a Virgo, you usually have the gift of the gab and great intelligence. However, that doesn't mean you're going to get through to another person if they're not willing to meet you halfway.

Friday 4th

Try not to get involved in an argument that no one can win. If you're feeling frustrated, go down to the gym or destress on a long walk. Some time apart could help a struggling relationship. Leave any hope of reconciliation as late as possible today. Forgiveness must be part of the picture.

Saturday 5th

Consider where there's a protective influence in your life. This might be another person who's got your best interests at heart, or perhaps it's a recent gift of money that's helped you tremendously. Focus your attention on what's positive in your life and steer clear of what's not.

Sunday 6th

Notice whether you experience a sense of relief today if you're spending time alone, or if you're away from someone who's a challenge in your life. This doesn't mean you're going to be apart forever. Don't blame yourself if you haven't been coping. Be kind to yourself instead.

Monday 7th

If you've taken a step back from a difficult situation or you've had a breather from a challenging relationship, it may feel as if there's a weight off your shoulders. Move into the new week being confident and positive about the future. Know that you can handle anything that materialises.

Tuesday 8th

You may experience a strong sense of freedom over the next couple of days. When you stop repeating the same behaviour, this can be liberating. Turn your attention towards your future goals and line up something fun and exciting, either by yourself or with a group of people.

Wednesday 9th

An on-off love relationship could be off again, or perhaps you've decided to let go of a relationship that's not progressing fast enough. It's important that you consider your feelings and ensure that you're not taken for granted. Be less impulsive both in love and with money.

Thursday 10th

Tune in to your intuition as this is a powerful time for inner knowingness. Ensure your head and heart agree when making decisions and help other people in your life to do the same. Be productive. Crack on with what you can achieve and avoid what you cannot.

Friday 11th

When a lot is going on in your personal life, this is bound to impact your work and sense of progress. Try and let go of any emotional issues and focus on your job. Keep coming back to what you know how to deal with and let go of a task or project that's beyond your abilities.

Saturday 12th

When it comes to a long-term relationship, aim for friendship first, intimacy second. Take baby steps towards reconciliation. It's a good day to meet up with old friends. Talk to someone you haven't seen for ages and time could run away with you. There's so much to catch up on.

Sunday 13th

Today's stars sprinkle some magic your way, especially if you're meeting up with people from your past. What you give you receive in return. If you want to open your heart to someone you loved previously, this is an ideal time to do so, as long as you don't have any preset expectations.

Monday 14th

Don't give yourself a hard time if you make a wrong move trying to help a child or lover first thing. When in doubt, say less, not more. Let the other person know you're there for them if they need you, but don't leap in trying to fix the situation. Be kind and caring to yourself too.

Tuesday 15th

You may be more moody than usual today and your emotions could run away with you. You might have a strong sense of justice and feel outraged if someone is behaving unfairly. As a Virgo, you have a strict ethical code and you expect other people to be equally respectful.

Wednesday 16th

You might feel restless today and you may have an itch that's impossible to scratch. Stay calm and don't act impulsively around other people. Where you would benefit from being spontaneous is by booking a holiday or a course of study.

Thursday 17th

If you're feeling bored or unsettled, don't take it out on other people today. If someone close is the reason why you're unhappy, consider what you can do to make things better. Start by looking at your wants and needs and whether they're being met. Be honest with yourself.

Friday 18th

You may find it hard to express yourself succinctly today. Yet speaking up in a manner that's logical and rational can facilitate understanding. You have Mercury, the planet of communication, in your star sign. Therefore, you're the one who's talking sense. Stand up for your rights.

Saturday 19th

You could indulge in some retail therapy today and enjoy yourself at the shops, or you might want to take some time out to be quiet and actively seek peace and harmony in your life. Walk in the fresh air, breathe deeply, meditate. Reconnect with your inner calm and a sense of repose.

Sunday 20th

If you're typical of your star sign, you're super sensitive to other people's moods. Today, it's worth considering how much you pick up on energies and how to release or shed them properly. Take steps to detox and cleanse your aura.

Monday 21st

You won't want anyone to disturb you today, especially if you're feeling peaceful after a quiet or relaxing weekend. If your energy is restored, find a calm space at work or at home to get on with your tasks. Learn how to block out the noise and other people's interferences.

Tuesday 22nd

Trying to juggle things so everyone gets a piece of your time could prove overwhelming. If in doubt, prioritise the people who need you the most. Remember to keep putting yourself first, at least some of the time, and focus on treats and pampering that boosts your spirits.

Wednesday 23rd

It's the start of your birthday month when you can pick up the pace on a personal level. If you've found it hard to get motivated recently or you've been hiding away, the planets are encouraging you to step out and be seen. The Sun's move into Virgo brings much-needed vitality and energy.

Thursday 24th

It's best to keep your feelings to yourself now as this is a retrograde phase when things aren't settled or final. You may be retracing your steps or mulling things over. Don't think that you have to try and sort everything out. Let things be until Mercury turns direct mid-September.

Friday 25th

When Mercury's in retreat, it's a wonderful time to do less not more. This is more important for you as Mercury is retrograde in Virgo. Book yourself on to a retreat or take a staycation and plan some time away from work, chores and the mundane side of life. Relax fully.

Saturday 26th

Make a conscious decision to let other people sort out their problems. Your default mode is to leap in and try to help. Be around happy children today and let their laid-back energy rub off on you. Learn to chill out more and let things be.

Sunday 27th

Money matters are under the cosmic spotlight from today as action planet Mars enters Libra and your money zone. This is your chance to get your finances on track and aim for balance and an easy flow. Put some firm rules and guidelines in place around a close relationship.

Monday 28th

Make the most of the long weekend and take some time out. Go on a day trip with the kids or have fun playing around with a new hobby. If you're abroad, you'll already be lining up your next holiday. Put the feel-good vibe back into life and do more of what you love.

Tuesday 29th

If you're back at work, your thoughts may be elsewhere. If a chance to take a last-minute holiday or a trip away comes up, grab it with both hands. If you're starting an educational course in September, it's worth considering all your options as something new could crop up.

Wednesday 30th

It might be hard to settle at work, especially if you're recently back from holiday. Set yourself some easy tasks today rather than attempting to tackle a major project. This evening, you may want to make time for love. A big full moon is looming and the theme is relationships.

Thursday 31st

Today's full moon highlights close relationships. This could be a romantic full moon when you lose yourself in the throes of love. Alternatively, someone close could let you down. It can go either way as the full moon could be revealing. Trust your intuition and let your emotions be your guide.

SEPTEMBER

. . . .

Friday 1st

The Sun remains in your star sign until September 22nd, which means it's your happy birthday month. When the planetary vibe is full-on this can be fun, social and empowering. There's no sense of moderation this weekend. You're either all in or ready to pull back.

Saturday 2nd

If someone in your life has been unusually quiet or you've been apart from the one you love, it's a good day to reach out and rekindle affections. A significant turning point is on the way, so trust your emotions and do what feels right. A private benefactor could give generously.

Sunday 3rd

If you hear about a trip that's been cancelled or there's a reason why a holiday can't go ahead, don't be too disappointed. There could be a better opportunity coming your way before long. Sometimes, you have to trust in life, as events in mid-September could prove to you.

Monday 4th

The planet of connection, Venus, turns direct today. For you, this could still be a hidden process, so perhaps you're away from the one you love or unsure of your feelings. Yet this could coincide with a shift in energy and it's a great date to reach out and connect.

Tuesday 5th

Your heart may not be in your work or your chores today if your thoughts are elsewhere. You could be excited because you're meeting someone who lives abroad for the first time, or you're waiting on exam results. The tension is palpable.

Wednesday 6th

There's a powerful planetary connection today in Virgo, which means you're the star sign of the moment. Pay attention to a synchronicity that emerges, especially around 11:11. Notice where you're ready to let go to create space for something new to come in. It's all about you.

Thursday 7th

It's hard to concentrate on work when there's so much going on in your personal life. Give yourself a break today and do less not more. If you're on holiday or enjoying a trip away, you're in tune with your stars. Your concentration may not be great, but your imagination is out of this world.

Friday 8th

Today's Sun-Jupiter connection favours risk-taking, big vision, excitement and adventure. You might mark this weekend's joyful astrology by saying yes to a new experience. The more you put into life, the more you could get back in return. Watch out for an offer you can't resist.

Saturday 9th

This isn't a weekend to stay at home and do nothing. Instead, do something special and line up an adventure or new experience. Your stars favour big and bold moves whether you're keen to live abroad or you're considering a sabbatical from work to pursue a life-long dream.

Sunday 10th

Be around friends who inspire you today. Walk the path less travelled and try out an alternative activity. If you're a typical Virgo, you'll be open to all things weird and wonderful and New Age interests are right up your street. You could attend a mind-body-spirit event.

Monday 11th

Take the pace slow when it comes to love and enjoy getting to know someone all over again. Don't jump the gun and rush into things. Give yourself until early October to make up your mind and see how the other person feels. You could be enjoying a long-distance relationship.

Tuesday 12th

If you've got a tight work deadline or you want to pay close attention to a hobby or project, shut the door to the outside world. This includes switching off social media, the news and all forms of technology. Take a digital detox and concentrate on inner work and self-mastery.

Wednesday 13th

It might seem as if you're playing a stuck record when it comes to one relationship in your life. If you keep running into the same issue, it doesn't matter how much you keep repeating yourself if the other person refuses to change. Stop talking and start thinking instead.

. . . .

Thursday 14th

Refocus your attention on your projects, personal goals and aims. Leave another person in your life out of the equation if you're getting nowhere with a joint venture or mutual activity. Tap back into your long-term goals. A new or exciting opportunity may come your way.

Friday 15th

Today's new moon and Mercury turning direct are a double blast of strong Virgo energy. Both events mean that it's an ideal weekend to start a new routine. This could help you get more organised at work or home, or start looking after your health and fitness.

Saturday 16th

It's important not to give all your energy away. This is an excellent weekend to put yourself first, at least some of the time, and focus on activities that boost your spirits. Choose carefully who you want to spend your time with. Ring the changes and start something new.

Sunday 17th

Your stars indicate that balance and harmony could restore your equilibrium. Decide what this means for you, what you want less of and what you need more of. Turn your attention towards money and the things in life you value highly. Consider your self-worth and ensure it's strong.

Monday 18th

Reach out to people in your life who you haven't talked to in a while. This is an excellent day for communication and getting to know someone close on a deeper level. Make time for conversation and don't rush headlong through life.

Tuesday 19th

A close relationship could be unravelling or confusing you. Bide your time if this is the case and don't make any sudden decisions. You can't see things clearly now, which means it's hard to make an honest judgement. If you're unsure what to do, make a list of pros and cons.

Wednesday 20th

You may learn a lot about yourself via other people's experiences. Rather than try to work out a complex issue on your own, reach out and ask for advice. This could be in a professional capacity or with people you see every day. Take care that your mood doesn't slump later on.

Thursday 21st

Prioritise your close connections, especially with a child or a lover. You might discover that someone close has hidden depths, or perhaps there's someone in your life who feels like a soulmate. Make a concerted effort to work on your relationships and listen well.

Friday 22nd

If you're feeling uncomfortable when you're at home or within your family, this is a sign that something's not right. Rather than deny what you're feeling, express your dissatisfaction honestly and openly. Being truthful about your situation could be all that's needed to shift the dynamic.

Saturday 23rd

Try not to get irritated or frustrated this weekend with the smaller details. Instead, focus on seeking peace and quiet in your life. Do less not more and choose where to focus your energy and attention. Money is one area of your life currently under the cosmic spotlight.

Sunday 24th

The moon is in your play and pleasure zone today, a sign to do more of what you love. Hang out with the kids, line up a lunchtime date or throw yourself into a much-loved hobby. Whatever you get involved in could become an obsession and you lose yourself completely in the process.

Monday 25th

If you haven't had a big holiday this summer, hopefully, you've had lots of little trips away or excursions close to home. Today feels lucky for you, so enter a competition or buy a raffle ticket. It's worth remembering that luck is an attitude and you have to work it to win it.

Tuesday 26th

A positive attitude would benefit you today, especially if you're keen to get a lot done. Be proactive around work and money matters. Start earlier than usual if it helps to make the right impression. You need to minimise all distractions so take yourself off somewhere quiet.

Wednesday 27th

When it comes to a romantic relationship, there can be no half measures. It's either on or it's off. One of you may have to decide whether you're ready to commit or you'd rather quit. Take relationships seriously today and don't let someone close off the hook if they refuse to participate.

Thursday 28th

You might not be happy with someone close, but there's a better chance of working things out today. Try not to be overly critical and choose your words carefully. What may help is to bring romance into your relationship. Line up a date night and agree to be amicable.

Friday 29th

It's a powerful full moon today that pits independence against a relationship. You may need to cut off emotionally and walk away from someone who's caused you pain in the past. Get rid of deadwood in your life, wipe the slate clean and allow new energy to flood in.

Saturday 30th

Money and emotions are closely linked and both are important in a relationship. If a partnership has become unequal in either of these areas, you're likely to be frustrated. Start by pointing out what's not working and consider what steps you can take to reach a compromise.

OCTOBER

. . . .

Sunday 1st

Your dreams rarely materialise without a plan. Spend some time today making a wish list and write down your next steps. If you can sense your inner entrepreneur calling, decide where you want to focus your attention over the coming month. Get ready to boost your finances.

Monday 2nd

Let go of any recent disappointments around love. Concentrate on what is working out rather than putting energy into what's not working out. If you're missing someone, line up a new adventure or experience for yourself. In fact, it's a good idea to do so whether you're in a couple or not.

Tuesday 3rd

If there's something you've been wanting to say to a child or lover, speak with conviction today. It's time to close the door on a situation that's dragged on over the last couple of months. Even if you agree to disagree, it's important to have the final word and move on.

Wednesday 4th

If you love your job or your daily routine, you'll be in seventh heaven today. There's an easy flow between your work and money zones, which suggests your contribution could be recognised. Some financial changes are on the way mid-month so ensure you stay on top of money matters.

Thursday 5th

Your ruling planet Mercury is on the move and enters your money zone today. Your stars indicate that creating equal agreements around money and sharing your finances could boost your current situation. Don't become financially dependent on another person, if you can help it.

Friday 6th

You may be swayed by a friend's influence today. They might want you to join in a social event or new experience. This is all well and good unless it's going to cost you more money than you can afford. Try to stick to your budget without putting a downer on the situation.

Saturday 7th

Today's stars could flag up a conflict around earnings or spending habits. This may be linked to a child or a lover. Take a step back if tempers flare. Agree to sort things out at a later date, especially if someone's anger gets the better of them.

Sunday 8th

Slow things down today so you can work things out in your head. If money is becoming an issue, try to come up with a solution and be prepared for a significant change next week. It doesn't mean that you'll lose out, but you may have to consider some new beginnings.

Monday 9th

It's not a promising picture for getting what you want financially today. Bear this in mind if you're trying to balance your finances, if you're keen to ask for a pay rise or demand money you're owed. Collaboration and goodwill may work better than an attacking attitude.

Tuesday 10th

Lovely Venus is in your star sign. This is a reminder that happiness and beauty don't have to cost the earth. Put your needs first and look after your body. This is particularly important if there's someone in your life who doesn't appreciate you the way they should.

Wednesday 11th

A situation could reach peak intensity today regarding a child or romantic relationship. You may have to take a step back and recognise that you can't fix everything. Be there for the ones you love but don't take over their lives. It's a tricky line to navigate, so trust your intuition.

Thursday 12th

Action planet Mars enters your communication sector today. This adds fire to your belly and a desire to take action. This is a confident Mars, great for networking, marketing and speaking up for yourself. If you're feeling strident, let other people hear what you have to say.

Friday 13th

Get things sorted out close to home, in your community or regarding your neighbours or siblings. You might step into a new role or position that requires a new level of responsibility. This would be a good weekend to arrange to meet your partner's relatives if they haven't met you yet.

Saturday 14th

Today's solar eclipse falls in your money zone today so keep on top of money matters and pay close attention to the flow of cash in your life. Eclipses often bring what's hidden to light. A new beginning could emerge from an ending.

Sunday 15th

Don't panic if your finances have changed significantly on the back of this weekend's eclipse. This could be the ideal opportunity to do things differently and look for a new way of earning money. Start by talking to the people in your life who you think might be able to help you.

Monday 16th

You may think it would be nice to be on holiday all the time. That's unlikely unless you are taking advantage of lucky Jupiter which is in your travel zone all year. If you aren't currently on the road, that doesn't mean there's nowhere to explore close to home. Try out some new local haunts.

Tuesday 17th

You may have become used to change over the last few years. Whether holidays got cancelled or a course of education was cut short, it's been a roller-coaster ride. You are wise to be flexible and adaptable still. Ensure you're ready to move fast if plans change once again.

Wednesday 18th

You may not see eye to eye with someone today, probably at home or within your family. Perhaps you disapprove of a relative's love life, or you don't like what someone's done to their appearance. Try not to let your high expectations get in the way of loving relationships.

Thursday 19th

You don't have to get on with everyone in your partner's family. That would be nigh on impossible now, so don't even try. Be realistic about who you like and notice who appreciates you. It's a promising day to discuss finances with a family member you trust inherently.

Friday 20th

Be wary if you're considering a deal that sounds great on paper but in reality is a high-risk investment. Steer clear and aim for financial security rather than financial risk. In any cash situation, it's important to read the small print and talk things through. Be thorough.

Saturday 21st

Emotional and financial affairs are linked now. Perhaps you need to find a way to back out of an agreement that's no longer working for you. Use your gift of the gab to negotiate well. In all money matters, aim to be amicable and diplomatic. Do what's best for everyone if you can.

Sunday 22nd

This is the time for some in-depth conversations when you leave no stone unturned. Go in deep, be analytical and winkle out hidden motivations on your part or regarding someone close. In your close relationships, it's the ideal time to tackle a taboo issue. Also, it's a lovely day for a first date.

Monday 23rd

The Sun's move into Scorpio today highlights your communication zone. When the Sun moves into this sector, you often find that life picks up the pace and you're busier than usual. Scorpio rules transport and connections as well as talking, reading and writing.

Tuesday 24th

This is a powerful week for making new contacts and deepening your connections. People matter, and you might choose to put someone else's feelings before your own. It would be a lovely day to get to know a neighbour better or catch up with a sibling. Reach out to others.

Wednesday 25th

When it comes to love, it's important to remember that beauty is more important inside than out. Don't let anyone else tell you otherwise and certainly don't let anyone criticise your looks. Be romantic, but be clear that you won't put up with game-playing or manipulative behaviour.

Thursday 26th

Your sex life could be on fire now. There's a passionate edge to your relationships and you may be willing to enter into a 'dangerous liaison'. As long as this works for both of you, enjoy the experience fully. Your star sign is red-hot on the inside, even if you have a cool demeanour.

Friday 27th

There's currently a link between money and love in your horoscope. You might be in a relationship with someone wealthy, or perhaps you're the one who's supporting someone close. Steer clear of those people who drain your finances and veer towards generosity and charitable concerns.

Saturday 28th

If you've experienced countless twists and turns over the last couple of years regarding travel or study, you get one more bite at the cherry today. It may take a bold move on your part to do something that's closely aligned with your beliefs and principles. Say yes to a big adventure.

Sunday 29th

When you have an eclipse cutting across your travel and study zones, it can mean that plans get cancelled or postponed. Yet your stars are urging you to overcome any challenges and expand your horizons. You may decide to volunteer abroad.

Monday 30th

It's wise to allow eclipse energy to calm down before you make a big decision. You are probably already aware that this isn't the time to be alone or quiet. You're being pulled into the world, whether to connect with others for social reasons or to step into a helping role.

Tuesday 31st

In affairs of the heart, it's a gorgeous date to be spontaneously romantic. Ask someone out on a date or reconnect with a person you met on a holiday romance. When you make bold choices, it will impress someone close to you. Be true to who you are and live your life fully.

NOVEMBER

....

Wednesday 1st

It might be hard to settle at work today, especially if romance is going well. Your heart may be elsewhere as your head tries to concentrate. This evening is perfect for taking the time to catch up with an old friend and tell them all about what's going on in your life.

Thursday 2nd

When it boils down to it, it's the people in your life who count. This might be something you're aware of at the moment if you have extra support or help. Alternatively, you may be enjoying relations with your neighbours or in your local community. Reach out and make new friends.

Friday 3rd

There's an expansive feel to your stars today, whether you're setting off on a big adventure or your heart is wide open. Sometimes, you have to take risks in life and not let fear or doubt hold you back. Keep your wits about you but ensure you embrace all that life has to offer.

Saturday 4th

Your ruling planet Mercury remains in Scorpio, which is great for heart-to-hearts, analysis and deep thinking. Today could be glitchy, however, with a few technological problems. There may be a clash of beliefs, so be wary of getting into a conversation that leads into tricky territory.

Sunday 5th

If your energy's in short supply, take some time today to recharge your batteries. You may have been doing too much recently, whether at work or out in the world. Slow things down for a while and you'll soon be raring to go once again.

Monday 6th

There's a lot of love in the air this week, so reach out to others and be open to receive. Today's stars promise a soulmate or heartfelt connection. Someone's offer of help or a kind gesture towards a child or lover could restore your faith in humankind. Be equally giving in return.

Tuesday 7th

Give in to Neptune's influence today – surrender to life, fall in love, allow yourself to cry, be by the sea – whatever's needed for you. It's a great day for a heart-to-heart and opening up about your emotions. The deeper you dive into a relationship, the more you get back.

Wednesday 8th

Finances are centre stage today so pay close attention to money matters. You could be sorting out finances or working out who's spending what and where your money goes. Keep on top of things and use your clever Virgo brain to get organised. Treat the ones you love.

Thursday 9th

You're wise to step in today to assist a child or lover. You may know exactly the right words to use and you're able to offer them insight and understanding. You're in tune with other people now. Trust your caring nature and reach out to counsel others or lend a listening ear.

Friday 10th

Your ruling planet Mercury enters Sagittarius today and your home and family zone. Talk things through with loved ones if you're dealing with a domestic issue. Try to find out what works best for everyone concerned. It's a good date to start thinking about property dealings or a home project.

Saturday 11th

Take care that you don't get involved in an overly-heated debate today. Tempers could fly, especially around your beliefs or principles. Take a step back if necessary and remember that everyone's different. Avoid taking any foolish risks if you're travelling or driving.

Sunday 12th

With the best will in the world, you may find it hard to understand another person's point of view today. Sometimes, other people's opinions or beliefs are opposite to your own and you can't change what you think. At least be generous, even if you have to agree to disagree.

Monday 13th

Today's new moon falls in your communication zone. This would be a lovely date to meet new people and use your gift with words to good effect. If there's someone you want to talk to, make it happen. You won't get on with everyone but at least you may discover who's on your side.

Tuesday 14th

Family is important to you now, so make time for them.
This may not please your other half if they think you're putting
yourself out or they don't want you to help. Yet it's right to do
what you want rather than let someone else's grumpy mood
hold you back.

Wednesday 15th

Meet up with a family member at lunchtime and go
somewhere special. It's an ideal day for a mutual support
session to re-establish the bonds of love. It's never easy if your
family don't get on with one another. Even if you have to see
them separately, do what's right for you.

Thursday 16th

Be around the people in your life who lift your spirits.
You might be delighted for a child if they have good news
about travel or study. If they're ready to spread their wings
and fly high, encourage them to do so. Alternatively, you
might be the one setting off on a journey.

Friday 17th

Whatever you feel passionate about, it's important to open
up and express yourself. One conversation might be about
romance or sex and you're ready to be daring and bold.
Be sociable this weekend and get involved.

Saturday 18th

You could start the weekend with all guns blazing, so be
attentive to what you say, discern carefully which issues to pick
up on and which to drop. You might be on your soapbox doling
out advice or information. Trust your intuition now as it could
prove invaluable to you.

Sunday 19th

Sunday is traditionally a day of rest, but it's unlikely that you're going to stop and do nothing today. You could be unusually busy, whether a lot's happening in your neighbourhood or you're catching up with chores and administration. Do yourself a favour and ask for some help or support.

Monday 20th

There might be a lot of gossip doing the rounds at work which could stop everyone from getting on. There's potentially frenzied excitement about current events. Aim to adopt a slower pace as the day goes on and take your lead from a partner who's the quiet, sensitive type.

Tuesday 21st

There's some lovely astrology taking place today which indicates good relations. You might witness someone being protective towards a child or be uplifted when you hear of an act of goodwill. This evening, stay out of the way and allow the course of true love to unfold.

Wednesday 22nd

The Sun enters your home and family zone today. This pulls you back towards your past, your childhood and where you're from. This would be a positive few weeks to complete a property deal or make a financial commitment that helps your family or strengthens your home.

Thursday 23rd

This is likely to be a busy time for you whether you're discussing a family get-together or you're in the midst of home renovations or a change of residence. Having to accommodate warring factions is rarely easy, but do your best to be civil with family members who don't get on.

Friday 24th

Action planet Mars enters your home and family zone today. This means that life at home and within your family will be extra busy from this weekend onwards. Mars promises passion, also potentially arguments. Notice who puts the brakes on a family project and get ready to react.

Saturday 25th

You may be required to step in and deal with a family issue today. If tempers flare, try not to take sides, however challenging. If a property deal runs up against an obstacle, you're right to be angry. If you wait until the coming full moon, you might see the situation more clearly.

Sunday 26th

Get up super early this morning and go on a big adventure. Not only will this do you the world of good but it will also help you gain a clear perspective on what's happening at home or within your family. Know that you aren't going to be able to please everyone so start by pleasing yourself.

Tuesday 5th

If a relationship is flourishing because you're communicating more, keep reaching out. Someone close may be seeing a counsellor or have some deep issues that need to be heard. Don't let other people get away with stuff and ensure that there's respect in a relationship on both sides.

Wednesday 6th

Romantic Neptune switches direction today, which could be emotional. This might be a time when love is blooming and flourishing, or there may be strong emotions around a partnership that need to be released. It's an ideal time to let go of resentment and practise forgiveness.

Thursday 7th

It's an excellent day to sort out finances, especially within the family. You might be discussing presents or who pays for what over the festive break. Be assertive and lead the negotiations. There's a lucky vibe too, so buy a raffle or lottery ticket.

Friday 8th

You may want to spend some quality time with a child or lover this weekend, especially if you're aware you may be apart over the festive season. If you're travelling to visit the one you love this weekend, you're in tune with your stars. Go with the flow and put other people first.

Saturday 9th

Don't be scared of expressing yourself this weekend but speak up about an issue that's bothering you. If you're talking at a work or social event, other people could love what you have to say. When you engage your emotions and speak with passion, it's easier for people to hear.

Sunday 10th

Being an earth sign, you require a love that's real. Make solid plans with your other half, firm up a relationship and bring love down to earth. It's all very well making promises and having good intentions but you need to see results.

Monday 11th

Focus on enjoyment and what makes you happy, and do more of it in the week ahead. Apply the same principle at your place of work. This is a good time to feel hopeful about love and focus on your long-term dreams. Love can take you out of yourself now, in a good way.

Tuesday 12th

Today's new moon lights up your home and family zone. This is an excellent time to start planning for the festive season and make arrangements. If you're a typical Virgo, you like to get organised in advance and you're a top list-maker. Get family members on board with your plans.

Wednesday 13th

Mercury turns retrograde today. It's best not to make any final decisions once Mercury's retreating through the zodiac. Instead, wait and see what occurs once Mercury's back up to speed in three weeks. This applies in particular to romance, children, creative projects, entertainment and fun.

Thursday 14th

This would be a good time to dive deep into a hobby or leisure activity. When Mercury's on go-slow, there's a theme of second chances and trying again with something you didn't master the first time around. If you're taking a long break from work, this suits your astrology perfectly.

Friday 15th

You may not be happy about what's happening with a child
in your life. Perhaps you've heard that you won't be seeing
someone special over the festive break, or you have to split
childcare between yourself and an ex, which is rarely easy.
Be honest about what you're feeling.

Saturday 16th

It's an excellent weekend to get organised whether you're
putting up the Christmas tree or working out the festive
schedule. You might decide to forego a social event or let your
other half take the day off. Ensure you do so generously and
don't make them feel wrong for doing so.

Sunday 17th

Today's stars can be romantic but there's a theme of losing
yourself. You may be disillusioned about love or swept away on
a tide of emotion. It's a sentimental time and you could be on a
trip down memory lane. Be there for someone close but ensure
you keep clear boundaries in place.

Monday 18th

You might be on a trip into your past today and be visiting
your childhood home. You could choose to travel a long way
if it means you get to see a child or someone you love. A lucky
encounter could mean you bump into someone you haven't
seen for years.

Tuesday 19th

If you've recently met someone new, ensure you ask the right questions today and get to know them better. You don't want to be heartbroken if you find out they're not on the same page. When it comes to love, open your heart because romance won't find you if you don't.

Wednesday 20th

There could be an upset today when you hear something you weren't expecting. Try and find the positives in the situation. Perhaps it means you have a lucky escape. If you hear about a sibling's relationship upset, reach out and be there for them, even if it means changing your plans.

Thursday 21st

Someone close may need you to be there for them. Put the ones you love first and offer whatever help or support you can. You might consider being a parent or adopting. If so, give yourself until the end of the year to make a final decision. Explore all your options carefully.

Friday 22nd

One key area of your life could bring you a lot of happiness now. There might be good news regarding children. Creative projects and the way you express yourself are highlighted too. Follow life's synchronicities and you may have a conversation that's life-changing.

Saturday 23rd

Communication planet Mercury retreats into your home
and family zone today. There's a theme of second chances,
so reach out and try and connect with someone you care
about. A sudden change of plan for the festive season may add
complexity but could turn out well in the end.

Sunday 24th

You must put people first and work second today. You might
be pulled in different directions as your sense of responsibility
kicks in. Ask for help or support if you can't get everything
done in time for the festivities tomorrow. Prioritise a
meaningful conversation this evening.

Monday 25th

The moon is in your career zone today so you may have said
yes to the festive shift, especially if you work in the caring
sectors. Yet love is prominent too, so be open-hearted and
enjoy all that the festivities bring your way. The more you give,
the more you receive in return.

Tuesday 26th

An argument could flare up first thing as tensions erupt.
If you've been enjoying a big family get-together, good
intentions to be amicable could go out of the window.
Ideally, catch up with your friends later on or be around the
person you feel most comfortable with.

Wednesday 27th

Today's full moon has a caring and compassionate vibe, although emotions will run high. If you've been invited to a social event, make the most of it. This could be a school reunion or a get-together with childhood friends. Put past disappointments to one side and embrace new love.

Thursday 28th

As a Virgo, it can be easy for you to put other people before yourself. This is something you're wise to change so you can learn to take good care of yourself. This may be more important today if you're faced with warring families. Don't feel obliged to get involved.

Friday 29th

You may be busy renovating, planning a move or decorating during the holidays. Happiness can be found at home. If you feel drawn back towards your past or someone you know from your childhood, follow your intuition. Home is where the heart is. Romance gets a look-in too.

Saturday 30th

You might need some downtime today, especially if you're socialising more than usual this week. Also, you want to be ready for New Year's Eve as the moon will be in your star sign on the night. This is your cue to do what pleases and not bow down to other people's needs.

Sunday 31st

You might be tempted to jump on a plane today, if you're able to, or go off and do something completely different. Ensure you fire some arrows high into the sky to line up some new adventures and experiences for 2024. Make a personal wish to welcome in the New Year.

Virgo

....

PEOPLE WHO SHARE
YOUR SIGN

PEOPLE WHO SHARE YOUR SIGN

. . . .

The valuable influence of warm and hard-working Virgoans can be felt in the smallest and largest of ways, from helping just one friend to serving the masses. From perfectionist actors like Keanu Reeves to Nobel Peace Prize winners such as Mother Teresa, Virgoans have the capacity to guide and inspire. Discover the public figures who share your exact birthday and see if you can spot the similarities.

24th August

Rupert Grint (1988), Chad Michael Murray (1981), John Green (1977), Alex O'Loughlin (1976), Dave Chappelle (1973), Ava DuVernay (1972), Marlee Matlin (1965), Stephen Fry (1957), Vince McMahon (1945)

25th August

Blake Lively (1987), Rachel Bilson (1981), Alexander Skarsgård (1976), Ben Falcone (1973), Claudia Schiffer (1970), Billy Ray Cyrus (1961), Tim Burton (1958), Gene Simmons (1949), Faustina Kowalska (1905)

26th August

Keke Palmer (1993), Dylan O'Brien (1991), James Harden (1989), Evan Ross (1988), Macaulay Culkin (1980), Chris Pine (1980), Amanda Schull (1978), Melissa McCarthy (1970), Mother Teresa (1910)

27th August
Alexa Vega (1988), Patrick J. Adams (1981), Aaron Paul (1979), Suranne Jones (1978), Sarah Chalke (1976), Mark Webber (1976), Tom Ford (1961), Peter Stormare (1953), Paul Reubens (1952), Barbara Bach (1947), Lyndon B. Johnson, U.S. President (1908)

28th August
Armie Hammer (1986), Florence Welch (1986), LeAnn Rimes (1982), Jack Black (1969), Sheryl Sandberg (1969), Shania Twain (1965), David Fincher (1962), Jennifer Coolidge (1961)

29th August
Liam Payne (1993), Lea Michele (1986), Carla Gugino (1971), Lenny Henry (1958), Temple Grandin (1947), James Hunt (1947), Iris Apfel (1921), Ingrid Bergman (1915)

30th August
Trevor Jackson (1996), Bebe Rexha (1989), Johanna Braddy (1987), Cameron Diaz (1972), Michael Chiklis (1963), Warren Buffett (1930), Ernest Rutherford (1871)

31st August
Sara Ramirez (1975), Chris Tucker (1971), Queen Rania of Jordan (1970), Tsai Ing-wen, President of the Republic of China (1956), Marcia Clark (1953), Richard Gere (1949), Van Morrison (1945), Georg Jensen (1866)

1st September

Zendaya (1996), Daniel Sturridge (1989), Chanel West Coast (1988), Boyd Holbrook (1981), Gloria Estefan (1957), Dr Phil McGraw (1950), Barry Gibb (1946), Lily Tomlin (1939)

2nd September

Alexandre Pato (1989), Zedd (1989), Salma Hayek (1966), Lennox Lewis (1965), Keanu Reeves (1964), Eugenio Derbez (1961), Mark Harmon (1951), Robert Shapiro (1942)

3rd September

Kaia Gerber (2001), Dominic Thiem (1993), Shaun White (1986), Garrett Hedlund (1984), Fearne Cotton (1981), Redfoo (1975), Charlie Sheen (1965), Malcolm Gladwell (1963), Jaggi Vasudev (1957)

4th September

Yannick Carrasco (1993), James Bay (1990), Beyoncé (1981), Max Greenfield (1979), Wes Bentley (1978), Mark Ronson (1975), Damon Wayans (1960), Dr Drew Pinsky (1958)

5th September

Giovanni Pernice (1990), Kat Graham (1989), Annabelle Wallis (1984), Carice van Houten (1976), Rose McGowan (1973), Michael Keaton (1951), Freddie Mercury (1946), Raquel Welch (1940), Jesse James (1847)

6th September
Lauren Lapkus (1985), Pippa Middleton (1983), Kerry Katona (1980), Naomie Harris (1976), Idris Elba (1972), Anika Noni Rose (1972), Macy Gray (1967), Swoosie Kurtz (1944), Roger Waters (1943), Jane Addams (1860)

7th September
Evan Rachel Wood (1987), Oliver Hudson (1976), Shannon Elizabeth (1973), Leslie Jones (1967), Toby Jones (1966), Eazy-E (1964), Gloria Gaynor (1949), Buddy Holly (1936)

8th September
Cameron Dallas (1994), Joe Sugg (1991), Avicii (1989), Wiz Khalifa (1987), P!nk (1979), David Arquette (1971), Martin Freeman (1971), Bernie Sanders (1941), Antonín Dvořák (1841)

9th September
Luka Modrić (1985), Zoe Kazan (1983), Michelle Williams (1980), Michael Bublé (1975), Adam Sandler (1966), Hugh Grant (1960), Colonel Sanders (1890), Leo Tolstoy (1828)

10th September
Ryan Phillippe (1974), Guy Ritchie (1968), Jack Ma (1964), Colin Firth (1960), Joe Perry (1950), Bill O'Reilly (1949), Cynthia Lennon (1939), Mary Oliver (1935), Karl Lagerfeld (1933)

11th September
Kygo (1991), Tyler Hoechlin (1987), Ludacris (1977), Taraji P. Henson (1970), Harry Connick Jr. (1967), Moby (1965), Scott Patterson (1958)

12th September

Connor Franta (1992), Alfie Allen (1986), Emmy Rossum (1986), Jennifer Hudson (1981), Ben McKenzie (1979), Paul Walker (1973), Hans Zimmer (1957), Barry White (1944), Jesse Owens (1913)

13th September

Niall Horan (1993), Ben Savage (1980), Fabio Cannavaro (1973), Stella McCartney (1971), Tyler Perry (1969), Dave Mustaine (1961), Jacqueline Bisset (1944), Roald Dahl (1916)

14th September

Jessica Brown Findlay (1989), Amy Winehouse (1983), Ben Cohen (1978), Andrew Lincoln (1973), Nas (1973), Sam Neill (1947), Margaret Sanger (1879)

15th September

Jenna Marbles (1986), Prince Harry, Duke of Sussex (1984), Tom Hardy (1977), Jimmy Carr (1972), Queen Letizia of Spain (1972), Tommy Lee Jones (1946), Agatha Christie (1890), William Howard Taft, U.S. President (1857)

16th September

Nick Jonas (1992), Alexis Bledel (1981), Amy Poehler (1971), Marc Anthony (1968), Molly Shannon (1964), Mickey Rourke (1952), Peter Falk (1927), B.B. King (1925), Lauren Bacall (1924)

17th September

Melissa Hemsley (1985), Flo Rida (1979), Anastasia (1968), Cheryl Strayed (1968), Kyle Chandler (1965), Narendra Modi, Indian Prime Minister (1950), John Ritter (1948), Jim Rohn (1930), Hank Williams (1923), Billy the Kid (1859)

18th September

Patrick Schwarzenegger (1993), Ronaldo (1976), Jason Sudeikis (1975), Xzibit (1974), James Marsden (1973), Jada Pinkett Smith (1971), Aisha Tyler (1970), James Gandolfini (1961), John McAfee (1945)

19th September

Danielle Panabaker (1987), Lauren Goodger (1986), Skepta (1982), Jimmy Fallon (1974), Sanaa Lathan (1971), Lita Ford (1958), Twiggy (1949), Jeremy Irons (1948), Adam West (1928)

20th September

Phillip Phillips (1990), Jon Bernthal (1976), Victor Ponta, Romanian Prime Minister (1972), Michelle Visage (1968), Kristen Johnston (1967), George R. R. Martin (1948), Sophia Loren (1934), Anne Meara (1929), Upton Sinclair (1878)

21st September

Jason Derulo (1989), Maggie Grace (1983), Nicole Richie (1981), Liam Gallagher (1972), Alfonso Ribeiro (1971), Luke Wilson (1971), Faith Hill (1967), Abby Lee Miller (1966), Shinzō Abe, Japanese Prime Minister (1954), Bill Murray (1950), Stephen King (1947), Leonard Cohen (1934)

22nd September

Daniela Ospina (1992), Tom Felton (1987), Thiago Silva (1984), Billie Piper (1982), Sue Perkins (1969), Andrea Bocelli (1958), Joan Jett (1958), Nick Cave (1957), Rosamunde Pilcher (1924)

23rd September

Anthony Mackie (1978), Karl Pilkington (1972), Jason Alexander (1959), Bruce Springsteen (1949), Julio Iglesias (1943), Romy Schneider (1938), Ray Charles (1930), Mickey Rooney (1920)